THINK LINK CREATE

Harnessing & Understanding The Universal Power Laws To Create Your Perfect Life

BY

GAVIN D HOLMES

Copyright © 2025 by
Gavin D Holmes

ALL RIGHTS RESERVED.

NO part of this book may be reproduced or transmitted in any form by any means, electronic or mechanical, including photocopying and recording, or by any information storage and retrieval system, except as may be expressly permitted in writing from the author.

Dedication

This book took me twelve years to write, and I'm grateful it did, as I learned so much while traveling the world as a trading professional and meeting thousands of people from different religions, cultures, and beliefs.

Firstly, I dedicate this book to all our wonderful customers of my trading businesses, TradeGuider Systems International and TradetoWin LLC, in over 35 countries. Thank you all for your support.

Next, I dedicate this book to you, the reader, for buying it. I hope you enjoy it and that it proves helpful to you.

Finally, I dedicate Think-Link-Create to my wonderful family: my wife of twenty years, Laura; my three children, Nathan, Olivia, and Ryan; and our two cocker spaniels, Lulu and Apollo.

I hope this book opens your mind, which is best used when it is open.

May your God bless you,

With best wishes and love,

Namaste.

Gavin Holmes

TABLE OF CONTENTS

Chapter 1 The Reason Why 1

Chapter 2 The Universal Power Laws Revealed 11

Chapter 3 The Power Of Visualization And Belief 18

Chapter 4 Food For Thought! 32

Chapter 5 Thought Vibration & Energy In The Material World 52

Chapter 6 The Power Of Words, The Inner Voice, And Emotional Responses 61

Chapter 7 Breaking The Cycle – Overcoming Negative Thought Patterns And Depressive Or Suicidal Thoughts 88

Chapter 8 The Power Of Self-Belief & Positive Actions 104

Chapter 9 As A Man Or Women Thinketh, So Shall They Reap 116

Chapter 10 The Universe Will Test You For The Next Step – Be Prepared 135

Chapter 11 Use Positive Words/Affirmations To Get Positive Results – Command Your Inner Voice – I Am… 145

CHAPTER 1

THE REASON WHY

The reason why I decided that now was the time to write this book is because after a near-death experience many years ago something happened that had a profound effect on me and changed my life dramatically, very much for the better.

I do not know where I first heard the term "Knowledge is Power" but after my near-death experience, some very strange things began to happen to me that began with me asking some serious questions about why I am I here on this earth and what is my purpose.

I cannot remember the circumstances that led me to a book called "Think and Grow Rich" by Napoleon Hill, however, I do remember as I read the book that I realized that for parts of my life, I had been drifting with no real sense of purpose. I knew the knowledge in this book was extremely powerful but what I found very difficult to at first accept is that our thoughts can manifest into something real in our lives.

It was during a very turbulent time in my life that Napoleon Hills book found its way into my possession. I had emigrated to the United States of America to start a business called TradeGuider, which I still own with my business partner Richard Bednall today. Starting any business is always going to be a challenge, but relocating to a completely different country and learning a new culture as well, was the biggest challenge of my life. I remember arriving in Chicago on the evening before Thanksgiving and getting to the apartment we had rented which was directly opposite the Sears Tower (now called the Willis Tower).

THE REASON WHY

It was early evening when I arrived and it was very cold and it had been snowing. As I opened the door to my new residence I remember a strong feeling of mixed emotions flowing through me. On one hand, I was extremely excited and looking forward to discovering all the wonderful things I had heard about America, and on the other hand, doubt was setting in as to whether I had made the right decision. Looking back, this was one of those times in life when you reach a crossroads and gut instinct kicks in. I knew there was no going back.

Within 6 months I met my wife Laura and we were married the following year. It was during the process of getting my green card that I went through an extremely difficult situation that made me depressed and negative. I am most definitely not a negative person and so this situation, which really got me down, was the catalyst for what I now realize is my life's destiny and purpose.

This is what happened. I had made an application for my green card and as part of this process, I had to undergo a medical exam, standard stuff. Everything was going very well at this point but then after a few months, I needed to leave the United States to see my son in England who was 6 years old at the time. I was advised that as I had an application for a green card going through I needed a special permit to leave the United States. If I left the United States without this permit I would have been seen to abandon my green card application and this would have cost us a lot in lawyer's fees and so I made the application for a permit to leave and re-enter the United States.

To cut a long story short, 18 months later I had still not got the permit despite writing numerous letters and making phone calls every week. I was banging my head against a brick wall trying to make sense of why this was happening to me. No one in the US immigration service seemed to have an answer and I was stuck in a process that seemed unresolvable.

Combined with this other negative things were happening to me and things seemed to be spiralling out of control. The business began to run out of money, arguments with business partners began and the final straw was a phone call from my son in England. He asked me why I did not want to come and see him and he said that I did not love him. To hear that over the phone in the situation I was in made me feel powerless, depressed, angry and frustrated. I was living a big pity party and all my feelings of resentment, anger and frustration were manifesting in situations around me. I needed an answer.

It was during this time that Napoleon Hills' book "Think and Grow Rich" and a book called "The Secret" by Rhonda Byrne were brought to my attention. I do not remember exactly how but I do now know that at the time I began to read them, I was at a big low point in my life and I needed answers. I remember to this day the moment I began to read "The Secret".

I was at my health club, The East Bank Club in Chicago, made famous because Barack Obama was also a member as well as Michael Jordon and Oprah Winfrey. It was a hot summer's day in July and I was at the outside pool and I began to read.

As I read each chapter I began to question much of what was being discussed in the book. Several times I was tempted to stop reading and say to myself what a load of rubbish, but something kept me going. My inner voice was playing games. It was a mini battle in my head, one side saying this information is rubbish and the other side saying persevere and you will be rewarded. Luckily for me, the side that said persevere and you will be rewarded won through, and this book is the result of that winning battle.

Initially, my greatest difficulty was trying to grasp the concept that thoughts are things that can manifest into your life experience. I could see from my own experience that when I was negative and down I seemed to keep getting more of the same, and when I was feeling great and positive I got more of the good things and I felt great, but could I control or at least influence what I was getting? Is there a universal law that applies to us all?

In books throughout history, the subject of the 'Law of Attraction' has been discussed. In fact, the book that Inspired "The Secret" was a book published in 1910 called "The Science of Getting Rich" by Wallace Wattles. "The Science of Getting Rich" preceded similar financial success books such as "The Master Key System" by Charles F. Haanel (1912).

In the 100 years since its publication, Wattles book has gone through many editions and remains in print from more than one publisher.

In essence, Law of Attraction refers to the idea that thoughts influence chance. The Law of Attraction argues that thoughts (both conscious and unconscious) can affect things outside the head, not just through motivation, but by other means. The Law of Attraction says that which is like unto itself is drawn. When I first began to find this information I was sent an email by one of our customers at TradeGuider. In the email, which thanked us for teaching him to trade and invest using a method called Volume Spread Analysis, he quoted an old Chinese proverb. I now know that what was happening to me as this information was received was all in this proverb.

"When the student is ready the teacher shall appear".

At that moment of my life, I was ready and I hope that you are ready to open your mind to the wonderful opportunities and connections that are all around you, right now, if you tune in to them. I will teach you how to tune in and focus your energy to get positive results in your life, starting now.

So I completed the book "The Secret" and it took me only two days to read completely. It was a Sunday night and so, the next question I asked myself was what do I really want and need, right now. Of course, the obvious answers I am sure many of you will think about would be more money, a bigger car, a bigger house etc., but at that moment, none of those things were as important as being able to leave the United States to see my son in England. I have always been good at visualizing things in my mind's eye which is an important part of using the Law of Attraction, however, as I learned there are other things that need to be done if you want to get positive results.

Gratitude for what you have now, even if you are going through a really tough time or a very dark period of your life, is very important. I was going through a very tough time and initially, I found being grateful somewhat difficult as my perception of my world was very negative at that moment. I remember that Sunday evening switching on the television and I watched a program about the famine in Africa and the struggles of human beings to just survive. I watched as the documentary explained how difficult it was to get fresh drinking water and how some children would not get a meal for days. I then looked at the wonderful apartment I was in, I looked out at the Chicago city view from my window and I watched as my wife cooked us dinner from our fully stocked fridge and at that moment I knew what gratitude was and I began to cry.

I went to bed that evening and decided it was time to make some changes and take positive action. One half of me was very excited at this new challenge and yet the other negative side was nagging at me with that inner voice, doubting and thinking this is a waste of time, this is all rubbish. I had nothing to lose and at this point, I was frustrated and negative. I knew there was only one thing that was going to stop that. It was me, I had to take massive action and change my direction. I knew that the knowledge I had been given was the key, now all I had to do was use it and prove to myself that it had value. Little did know I had started a chain of events that would change my life in many positive ways that have not stopped and keep going.

The next morning my waking thought was of my son in England and that I really needed the documentation to leave the United States. I started my day not in the usual way which was to worry about the day ahead and think of issues that were consuming me. No, this day I thought of all the things I have to be grateful for and decided a good start would be to write them down on paper and take a look. Amazing, I was up to twenty and still going. This commitment to writing had a profound effect on me because it allowed me to focus on the moment. I realized that I had been given gifts at birth that I took for granted. I was happily married, I had a great place to live, a great social and professional network and much to look forward to, so why did I feel like I felt. I was attracting negative situations without being conscious I was doing it as I now know.

So as you read this book I want you to get the very best from this knowledge.

Note the points below and prepare your mind, for this book is written to open your mind with infinite opportunities for you.

1. Your mind is like a parachute, best used when it is open. Please open your mind and see what happens. Miracles exist, but we must create them.

2. Have faith. As the great Steve Jobs said, "You can't connect the dots looking forward; you can only connect them looking backwards. So you have to trust that the dots will somehow connect in your future. You have to trust in something — your gut, destiny, life, karma, whatever. This approach has never let me down, and it has made all the difference in my life".

3. Believe in yourself. You have unlimited power if you know how to channel your energy in the right direction. This book will give you strategies and tools to connect with your higher self so you can benefit immediately as well as long term.

4. These were the final words from the great Steve Jobs and they have great meaning and an underlying message for us all and these words made a profound difference to my perspective on life as I knew it.

STEVE JOBS'S FINAL WORDS FOR US ALL

"I have come to the pinnacle of success in business.
In the eyes of others, my life has been the symbol of success.
However, apart from work, I have little joy. Finally, my wealth is simply a fact to which I am accustomed.
At this time, lying on the hospital bed and remembering all my life, I realize that all the accolades and riches of which I was once so proud, have become insignificant, with my imminent death.
In the dark, when I look at the green lights, of the equipment for artificial respiration and feel the buzz of their mechanical sounds, I can feel the breath of my approaching death looming over me.

Only now do I understand that once you accumulate enough money for the rest of your life, you have to pursue objectives that are not related to wealth.
It should be something more important:

For example, stories of love, art, dreams of my childhood.
No, stop pursuing wealth, it can only make a person into a twisted being, just like me.
God has made us one way, we can feel the love in the heart of each of us, and not illusions built by fame or money, like I made in my life, I cannot take them with me.
I can only take with me the memories that were strengthened by love.
This is the true wealth that will follow you; will accompany you, he will give strength and light to go ahead.

Love can travel thousands of miles and so life has no limits. Move to where you want to go. Strive to reach the goals you want to achieve. Everything is in your heart and in your hands.

What is the world's most expensive bed? The hospital bed.
You, if you have money, you can hire someone to drive your car, but you cannot hire someone to take your illness that is killing you.

Material things lost can be found. But one thing you can never find once you have lost it, is life.

Whatever stage of life where we are right now, at the end we will have to face the day when the curtain falls.

Please treasure your family love, love for your spouse, love for your friends...

Treat everyone well and stay friendly with your neighbours".

Moments after speaking these words, that he had asked to be written down, Steve Jobs, aged 56, passed away.

Life is precious, it is a gift and we must always remember that.

THE REASON WHY

These lyrics are taken from the song by Talk Talk, "Lifes What You Make It", the words are very powerful and meaningful.

We are not perfect – but we can try to be – words are powerful.

Baby, life's what you make it
Can't escape it
Baby, yesterday's favourite
Don't you hate it
Baby, life's what you make it
Don't backdate it
Baby, life's what you make it
Beauty is naked
Baby, life's what you make it
Celebrate it
Anticipate it
Yesterday's faded
Nothing can change it
Baby, life's what you make it

Are YOU in control of YOUR World or is THE "World" controlling YOU?

THE REASON WHY

YOU are powerful, believe it

YOU are part of creation, so be creative, it's your destiny, enjoy it.

What you see every day in the "media" – our main source of information!!

"If you do not read the newspaper you are uninformed. If you do read the newspaper you are misinformed"

– Mark Twain.

CHAPTER 2
THE UNIVERSAL POWER LAWS REVEALED

I was asked at a recent seminar I was holding if I believed in miracles? It was a question that came out of the blue but without really thinking I replied, "Well the very fact that I am able to walk around this planet we call Earth as it travels around the sun at a speed of fifty-five thousand miles an hour thanks to the law of gravity is a miracle in itself, so the answer is yes I do".

The dictionary definition of gravity is interesting when you think about it.

1. Physics

    a. The natural force of attraction exerted by a celestial body, such as Earth, upon objects at or near its surface, tending to draw them toward the centre of the body.

    b. The natural force of attraction between any two massive bodies, which is directly proportional to the product of their masses and inversely proportional to the square of the distance between them.

    c. Gravitation.

2. Grave consequence; seriousness or importance: They are still quite unaware of the gravity of their problems.

3. Solemnity or dignity of manner.

Do I understand what the universal law of gravity actually is and the science behind it, unfortunately not, I do not know. I do, however, accept that there is a hidden force that is always working and is part of living as a Human Being, and so I do not question why and how the force works, I just accept the fact that this invisible force is at work on this planet constantly.

There are many things we take for granted in our lives, especially in the Western world. Much of the population does not understand and does not need to understand how things work. Take for example electricity and light. When I switch on my lights at home I know that it is electricity that is powering the bulbs. I accept this as normal but our civilization only started to use electricity in the last few hundred years. The reason I point this out is because I believe there are many more things we are going to invent and learn in the next hundred years and beyond and increased knowledge, acceptance and understanding of the universal power laws will have a dramatic and positive effect on our world.

In this book, I am not going to discuss every universal law that I am aware of although I have listed below the most common universal laws. I am going to focus instead on the key universal laws that I have used very successfully with strategies for you to use quickly and effectively in your life RIGHT NOW.

Below is a list of universal laws in no particular order of preference. Please do not feel overwhelmed by all these universal laws. They are all at work around you constantly but certain people make use of and understand all or some of these laws more than others.

If you have read religious scripture you will find that many of these laws have been written about for thousands of years.

The Law of Harmony

The Law of Reincarnation and Karma

The Law of Divine Oneness

The Law of Non-Resistance

The Law of Cause and Effect

The Law of Rhythm

The Law of Relativity

The Law of Sacrifice

The Law of Forgiveness

The Law of Obedience

The Law of Receiving

The Law of Wisdom

The Law of Grace

The Law of Soul Evolution

The Law of Bodhisattva

The Law of Vibration

The Law of Free Will

The Law of One

The Law of Manifestation

The Law of Conscious Detachment

The Law of Gratitude

The Law of Fellowship

The Law of Resistance

The Law of Unconditional Love

The Law of Magnetic Affinities

The Law of Abundance

The Law of Divine Order

The Law of Compensation

The Law of Perpetual Transmutation of Energy

The Law of Action

The Law of Correspondence

The Law of Reflection

The Law of Forgiveness

The Law of Supply and Demand

The Law of Effort Vs Result

The Law of Attraction

The Law of Gender

The Law of Polarity

The Law of Inspired Action

Sods Law!!

It would be fair to say that before 2006 I knew little or nothing about the importance of our belief systems and had never heard of the Law of Attraction or, in fact, had even considered that universal laws, apart from the law of gravity, were important in our lives or indeed had any real effect on our lives, and things that happen to us.

An event during 2006 led me to some information that had a profound effect on my life from the moment I discovered it. Whilst the event itself is unimportant, what I discovered is extremely important. What I discovered is that what we think about will have a great effect on what actually happens to us in our lives, good or bad. Now we all have thoughts, and we all have that inner voice that talks to us, but have you ever stopped to consider what that voice is and why it is there? I certainly never did until 2006, in fact, it meant little to me other than I had thoughts--- some made me feel good, some made me feel very good, but some made me feel bad, some made me feel very bad.

So what is the 'Universal Law of Attraction'? There are many definitions of the Law of Attraction and indeed, there are many great books on the subject.

The phrase "Law of Attraction", used widely by New Thought writers refers to the idea that thoughts influence chance. The Law of Attraction argues that thoughts (both conscious and unconscious) can affect things outside the head, not just through motivation, but by other means. The Law of Attraction simply states that like attracts like.

Most recently, the claims of the Law of Attraction are seemingly being supported by a growing body of scientific evidence and opinion, leading to the conclusion that there remains much research needs to be carried out on this subject in order to enhance our understanding of the universe.

In 1910 Wallace Wattles wrote a book called "The Science of Getting Rich" (which was the inspiration for the bestselling book "The Secret" by Rhonda Byrne). This is one of the books in my recommended reading section at the end of the book and is also listed on www.tradingintheshadow.com. Wallace Wattles stated:

"The scientific use of thought consists in forming a clear and distinct mental image of what you want; in holding fast to the purpose to get what you want; and in realizing with grateful faith that you do get what you want."

A consistent theme with Wallace Wattles and many other great luminaries of their time is "The insistence that by using our brains and our own thoughts in a harmonious manner with the positive aspects of the universe, we can bring about great and beneficial changes in our lives."

Wattles wrote, "Everything works under the same laws, yesterday, today and forever".

He was adamant that we create our own lives, and that does not happen if we sit on our backsides waiting to win the lottery or find some hidden treasure!!!

My Definition of The 'Universal Law Of Attraction' Is This:

The universe we inhabit as human beings is made up of energy forces that are only now starting to be understood by mankind.

One of the most fundamental universal forces that we accept as scientific fact began as an Aristotelian hypothesis, was rebutted by a more accurate experiment by Galileo, and finally successfully mathematically postulated and hypothesized by Isaac Newton. As a result, gravity came to be accepted as a scientifically proven natural law.

In regard to the Law of Attraction, we all have the power of thought, and all creative things in human life start from a thought. Thoughts come into manifestation in our lives by us taking positive action on positive thoughts (and unfortunately you have the opposite, which is negative action taking on negative thoughts).

A manifestation is something that you have created that appears in your life as the result of your thoughts and actions. Many, if not all who read this book will have experienced the feeling of déjà vu – that moment in time when you experience a feeling and an emotion that makes you feel as though you have been in that very same moment before. Paying attention to your thoughts and your feelings and being aware of the power of your ability to create what you want, (and also what you don't want!!) is the key to having an enjoyable and happy life.

In 1912, Charles Haanel wrote "The Master Key System" that gave practical techniques for using the Law of Attraction to manifest love, harmony, happiness, abundance and fulfilment from life. His book inspired further great works from Napoleon Hill (author of Think and Grow Rich) and Ernest Holmes (The Science of Mind).

The Law of Attraction has been discussed in many texts and books going back hundreds of years but has recently become more mainstream due to the work of Esther and Jerry Hicks, Rhonda Byrne, Michael Lossier, Dr. Joe Vitale (to name a few great authors), and Oprah Winfrey, who has featured the subject on her popular daytime talk show.

Like the Universal Law of Gravity, which took from the time of Aristotle until the modern day to be scientifically proven, forward thinkers would regard the Law of Attraction as scientifically nascent. Scientists are getting closer and closer to discovering the true power of the human brain, and most importantly, the POWER OF THOUGHT.

The common perception even among the professionally trained community is that mind and brain are synonymous. However, in reality, the two entities are separate.

Wattles wrote, "Everything works under the same laws, yesterday, today and forever".

He was adamant that we create our own lives, and that does not happen if we sit on our backsides waiting to win the lottery or find some hidden treasure!!!

CHAPTER 3
THE POWER OF VISUALIZATION AND BELIEF

The Law of Attraction has been discussed in many texts and books going back hundreds of years but has recently become more mainstream due to the work of Esther and Jerry Hicks, Rhonda Byrne, Michael Lossier, Dr. Joe Vitale (to name a few great authors), and Oprah Winfrey, who has featured the subject on her popular daytime talk show.

Like the Universal Law of Gravity, which took from the time of Aristotle until the modern day to be scientifically proven, forward thinkers would regard the Law of Attraction as scientifically nascent. Scientists are getting closer and closer to discovering the true power of the human brain, and most importantly, the POWER OF THOUGHT.

The common perception even among the professionally trained community is that mind and brain are synonymous. However, in reality, the two entities are separate.

This next section is taken from chapter nine of my first book, "Trading in the Shadow of the Smart Money" and is a great example of the power of belief and visualization which I shall discuss later in the book.

HOW TO USE BELIEF AND THE UNIVERSAL LAW OF ATTRACTION TO TRADE AND INVEST

In some ways, this will be the most difficult and even most controversial chapter to write, but in other ways, for me, this was going to be the easiest. It would be fair to say that before 2006 I knew little or nothing about the importance of our belief systems and had never heard of the Law of Attraction or, in fact, had even considered that universal laws, apart from the law of gravity, were important in our lives or indeed had any real effect on our lives, and things that happen to us.

An event during 2006 led me to some information that had a profound effect on my life from the moment I discovered it. Whilst the event itself is unimportant, what I discovered is extremely important. What I discovered is that what we think about will have a great effect on what actually happens to us in our lives, good or bad. Now we all have thoughts, and we all have that inner voice that talks to us, but have you ever stopped to consider what that voice is and why it is there? I certainly never did until 2006, in fact, it meant little to me other than I had thoughts- some made me feel good, some made me feel very good, but some made me feel bad, some made me feel very bad.

So what is the 'Universal Law of Attraction'? There are many definitions of the Law of Attraction and indeed, there are many great books on the subject. The phrase "Law of Attraction", used widely by New Thought writers refers to the idea that thoughts influence chance. The Law of Attraction argues that thoughts (both conscious and unconscious) can affect things outside the head, not just through motivation, but by other means. The Law of Attraction simply states that like attracts like. Most recently, the claims of the Law of Attraction are seemingly being supported by a growing body of scientific evidence and opinion, leading to the conclusion that there remains much research needs to be carried out on this subject in order to enhance our understanding of the universe.

In 1910 Wallace Wattles wrote a book called "The Science of Getting Rich" (which was the inspiration for the bestselling book "The Secret" by Rhonda Byrne). This is one of the books in my recommended reading section at the end of the book and is also listed on www.tradingintheshadow.com. Wallace Wattles stated: "The scientific use of thought consists in forming a clear and distinct mental image of what you want; in holding fast to the purpose to get what you want; and in realizing with grateful faith that you do get what you want." A consistent theme with Wallace Wattles and many other great luminaries of their time is "The insistence that by using our brains and our own thoughts in a harmonious manner with the positive aspects of the universe, we can bring about great and beneficial changes in our lives."

Wattles wrote, "Everything works under the same laws, yesterday, today and forever". He was adamant that we create our own lives, and that does not happen if we sit on our backsides waiting to win the lottery or find some hidden treasure!!!

Like the Universal Law of Gravity, which took from the time of Aristotle till the modern day to be scientifically proven, forward thinkers would regard the Law of Attraction as scientifically nascent. Scientists are getting closer and closer to discovering the true power of the human brain, and the POWER OF THOUGHT.

The common perception even among the professionally trained community is that mind and brain are synonymous. However, in reality, the two entities are separate. The brain 140 on the one hand is organically biochemical, and the mind is a psychic organ. Seemingly, the riddle to understanding the Law of Attraction lies in understanding the "glue" that joins both mind and body. Science is now beginning to show us that through the process of biochemical generation of electricity in the body, this electrical current joining body and mind must be capable of emitting a field of electrical energy which radiates from the body when activated by thought processes. Just as light has recently been discovered to consist of sub-atomic particles called photons, it is not unreasonable to believe that thoughts could very soon be proven to consist of electromagnetic radiation, and therefore subject to known scientific laws. Such a postulation and hypothesis, if proven, will move the Law of Attraction from the esoteric realm into that of scientifically proven fact.

The Law of Attraction would then make sense from such a basis in fact and will be supported by other scientific laws like synchronicity and resonance, which would explain why "like attracts like" etc. Taking the subject somewhat deeper, the brain consists of four main parts, but for the purposes of this discussion, the largest part is of interest to us, namely the cerebrum. The neo-cortex of the cerebrum is its surface area, and it is in this neo-cortex that science tells us that there exist billions of neurons. It is believed that these neurons are constantly sending electrical energy not only to the rest of the cerebrum, but also to other parts of the brain, and therefore by didactic reasoning, to other parts of the body.

It is these scientific postulations and facts concerning the neuronal electrical activity that give us a deeper look into, and understanding of the Law of Attraction when linked to our current scientific understanding of electromagnetic radiation and the fields it produces. Now, the interesting thing is that it is scientifically considered that the cerebrum is the area of the brain of the brain where thoughts originate. It's also the seat of our abilities to think, read, write, speak, mathematize, and create, e.g. musical compositions and works of art etc. More importantly to the subject of the Law of Attraction, the cerebrum is the area responsible for cognitive thoughts, memory and intelligence, and psychic phenomena. Hence, the Law of Attraction seemingly is a manifestation of a person's using the power of thought and feeling to influence circumstances that have a desirable outcome for you in your life by taking action on those positive thoughts and feelings so that the desired result can be attained.

It also means that if negative thoughts come in, you learn to manage those thoughts and not take negative action that may, or probably will, have a negative result in your life 141 Therefore, on a level of cause and effect, it would seem reasonable to assume that the positive electro-magnetic radiations that we pulsate (positive thought) would seek to find resonance with similar radiations, and when found, produce the summation resonance which manifests the result as a positive outcome. In other words, the goal achieved! Interestingly, the theory of the effect of electromagnetic radiation seems to also have some basis for understanding in Chaos Theory. The theory argues that tiny local changes (e.g. your thoughts) can produce large changes in your circumstances through the electromagnetic radiation of your thoughts to produce by resonance, the object of your thoughts, which could be either positive or negative goals.

To try and explain Chaos Theory, the famous "butterfly effect" postulates that the beating of butterfly wings can lead to a hurricane by way of the minuscule turbulence it generates could predictably lead to a critical combination of air pressure changes, resulting in the hurricane. Whether that's true or not is yet to be proven, but it's an interesting thought! The universe, as we know it, is too vast for the average human being to comprehend or even think about. Even our own planet is vast and when we start to think about our own lives on this vast planet we can feel inferior, insecure and unimportant, but that could not be further from the truth, as we are all equally important. The universe has been created by a higher power, a universal source of energy that means many things to many different people, depending on their upbringing, their country, their religion, and their belief system.

Whether you believe in God, or an existence of a higher being or power is, of course, a choice we all have and I can only speak from my own experience. I believe that we are all interconnected with that higher power, which I call God, and that at any time we can draw inspiration, ideas and assistance when we need it if we are taught how. If you examine the Chinese philosophy of Yin Yang (or "yin and yang" as we call it in the Western world), it is used to describe how polar or seemingly contrary forces are interconnected and interdependent in the natural world, and how they give rise to each other in turn. Opposites will therefore only exist in relation to each other. Everything is in perfect balance, which is why we have good and bad things going on in the world at any time.

Unfortunately, there is no news in good news, so when we watch our televisions or read our newspapers, all we see is bad news and that makes us feel that the world is in a big mess, but it is not at all, it is an intelligent design that has created this and so surely we should work with that intelligence to create better lives for ourselves and those around us. If we believe that the very base root of our creation consists of our physical bodies charged with electrical and spiritual energy, it makes sense that our thoughts will assist 142 us to connect with the ultimate energy source. The energy that created the universe also created life as we know it. Imagine that you are a receiver and also an emitter of energy, and you have states of high energy and also states of low energy. Many people who are depressed or suffer from depression complain of having little or no energy. People who have high energy and who make people feel good when they are around them are said to give off a "good vibe".

The word vibe refers to vibrational energy and many books have suggested that human beings have different vibrational energy levels that can be attained and will attract like vibrational levels as the ones they are giving out. It seems that like would attract like – bringing us round circle back to the Law of Attraction! The subject is both vast and interesting but outside the scope of this book. So why has this concept been discussed in a book about VSA and chart reading, you may ask? Well, because when you trade and invest, you want to make money, hopefully, lots of money, but in order to make money you must first attract that money by thinking positively and harmoniously with the universe. This will give you a greater chance of attaining your individual goals, be it financial or something else. By setting out your financial goals and focusing on them with clarity of thought, expectation of results with realistic goals, and then using the Law of Attraction to help manifest them in your life, you will be well on your way to finding true contentment and happiness, and if I can do it as I have done, then anyone can achieve it.

Hopefully, by sharing my thoughts and research on the subject, it will go a long way in convincing you of the reasonably possible scientific basis of the Law. The Power Of Visualization - An Example In 1999 I had the good fortune to meet Paul Avins, who at the time had just started his own consultancy firm and now has gone on to be one of the UK's leading business coaches. (www.paul-avins.com). Paul introduced me to the concept of visualizing success and he suggested I go with him to a seminar run by Tony Robbins, a well-known and well-respected teacher and author in the personal development field. (www.tonyrobbins.com). I have to say I was extremely sceptical when I paid over $2000 to find out that part of this process was walking over hot coals shouting out "Cool moss!" as I did it, but the whole experience was an eye-opener for me. Tony Robbins and Paul Avins explained that to make something positive happen in your life you must take MASSIVE ACTION. That what holds many human beings back -

something called 'self-limiting beliefs'.

I want to thank Tony and Paul for their insights which have helped me write this book and decided to cover this subject to help enlighten the reader. A self-limiting belief often starts with a word that begins a sentence you are telling yourself. Sentences may start with:

• I cannot • I will not • It does not • I am not sure • I doubt • Maybe • I don't know • It is impossible • I am afraid The above are very common things that traders and investors think as they are about to pull the trigger. Positive Belief Systems Result In Positive Manifestations When you begin your day as I do, by making positive suggestions and thoughts, miraculous things happen.

The feeling of déjà vu happened to me in a very strong way back in 2010 at the Traders Expo in New York. In 2007 I had a very powerful thought that at some point in the future, I would be trading live in front of a large audience and I would make a winning trade and explain all the VSA principles at work. As time went on I began to play out in my mind's eye exactly what I would be wearing, what the trade would look like and what would happen as I executed the trade. Then, I got a call in December 2009, and that is what happened!! These pictures are of me trading live at the New York Trader's Expo at the Trader's Challenge, in 2010. I was able to successfully make a profitable trade when I identified one of my favourite set-ups, a 'Test In A Rising Market'. I took the trade based on a clear VSA set-up that appeared on the five-minute and three-minute charts of the E-Mini NASDAQ.

Using positive sentences in your thoughts will result in positive outcomes, but what I noticed is it does not happen instantly, it comes over time the more you continue to think this way until it almost becomes second nature. Visualize in your mind what you really want. I have heard many practitioners of the Law of Attraction produce a vision board made up of pictures and images that they would want in their lives. These can be very helpful in focusing your thoughts in a positive direction.

THE POWER OF VISUALIZATION AND BELIEF

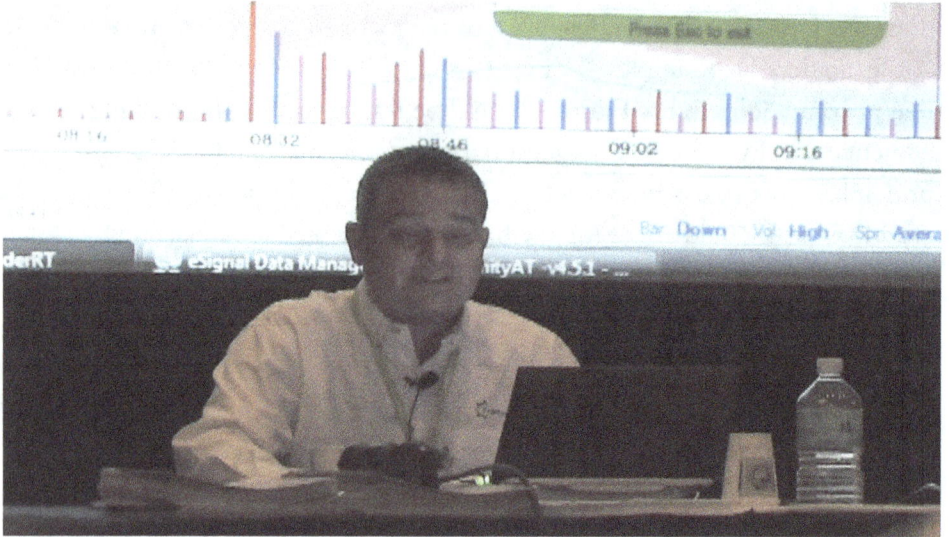

Some positive belief statements that go with the positive visualization start with: • I can • I will • I am a winner • It is possible • Yes • I am sure • Definitely

The second thing we now must have in order to succeed in the trading and investing world is BELIEF. In the last chapter, we talked about the top sportsmen and women practising to be the best, but if you hear interviews with all these stars, the word 'belief' will pop up all the time. I know. I listen to it. Today as I write this, my soccer team Southampton, also 145 known as

The Saints (a team from the south coast of England), was promoted to a higher division. In recent interviews, the manager talked about the players' desires and beliefs to get promoted, and they got what they deserved today. Well done, Saints. So is belief important if you are trading and investing? Well, I would like to acknowledge and thank TradeGuider customer Rakesh Kumar, who very kindly allowed me to use his writings from an e-mail he sent me on November 18th, 2005. I have treasured it ever since and sent it to our customers who lack belief. The first part is the actual body of the e-mail Rakesh sent me, and the second part was the attachment, which was a Word document. I hope this inspires you as it did me: Hi, Gavin, I once again looked at the chart of the week and thought I would bring to your notice a couple of crucial points.

Once again, like yesterday, the market was gapped up trapping and catching all those buy-stop losses of those who were shot overnight, this was followed by the test of our patience to the limit during the extended distribution period and then bang- prices marked down to lock in all the suckers. Look at the moves on DAX, 35-45pts ($800-1000) compared to just a few points on ES-mini. As I said this market is excellent for trading. Would be a good idea to have the last two days analysed as charts of the week (buying climax) by Tom & Sebastian and then archived with the existing one. (Selling Climax)

Now in the present chart of the week, most would focus on the chart, however there are a few gems of comments by Tom on "Belief" a) You have to believe these underlying principles b) You have to believe that these markets work on supply and demand. c) You have to believe that these markets reflect the consensus of professional opinion at that time. Also in his seminars many times he remarks "If you don't believe me check it out for yourself" Now hardly anybody pays attention to these words, but I can assure you if you go through the interviews of super traders in Market Wizards, it will become evident that a total belief in a particular strategy and having the discipline to implement that strategy and accepting the probability of the strategy with every cell in the body is at the heart of the success of these super traders. These guys have stuck to simple strategies and their responses have become automatic, there is no conflict in their mindset. Just like driving, initially, we have that fear of accidents coupled with the motivation to learn; hence the anxiety and stress. However, with practice, this conflict is resolved. Trading which is the most unique profession in the world is of course in a different league.

Humans are just not hard-wired for trading, period. (to deal with uncertainty continuously).

Every trading strategy based around any indicator with say over 50% probability would work if a trader totally believed in it and applied it with discipline, however in 90% of the cases this will not happen simply because that crucial transformation based on belief has just not happened, hence as soon as we are in front of the screen, anxiety, conflict sets in. With indicator-based strategy, we don't know "WHY" it is working and that causes conflict, deep down there is that nagging disbelief. Right from birth we have always been seeking answers to "WHY" and this is carried into the trading arena.

There is nothing like emotion-free trading. The right belief structure has to be in place to resolve the conflict in the mind, uncertainty against total belief in our ability to read the market. 5. This right belief structure can be gained by understanding VSA principles, which govern all the price patterns, price action and the derivative indicators thereof, i.e. that is the truth of the market. It provides the answer to "WHY" which is what the human mind seeks. Once that is fully accepted into the psyche, the conflict is resolved, emotions can be managed, (e.g. during driving, we still have emotions, we do not drive around like zombies, but we manage them, mind you nowadays this could be argued, with all that evidence of road rage on our streets) trading would then become like driving a Bentley, and this is the only software in the world which allows a trader to achieve that mindset.

Best, Rakesh --End of letter-- Now here is the attachment Rakesh sent me:

Why you can't win at trading? (10% do) What sets the 90% apart from the 10%? Why is one person seemingly able to effortlessly take profits from the market almost on a daily basis and yet another person trading the same market at the same time will be suffering consistent losses? Already even at this stage, the 90% will be thinking that the 10% guys have better indicators or even a holy grail trading strategy. On close examination of the 10% however, it will ALWAYS be found that they often use the same software, the same data, the same indicators and often trade at exactly the same time. If this is the case (and it is) then surely they must be gurus, they must have the 'Midas' touch, the golden key etc.... Well sorry to disappoint you, but once again this is simply not true, the 10% group consists of traders with many years of experience trading as part of huge organizations and also the one man/woman in his home trading from a simple PC screen. In reality, they are a pretty 'ordinary' lot.

They do have one consistent common factor however, which is usually revealed within 5 minutes of meeting them. They are also more often than not the most genuine of people who take a genuine interest in other traders. When one of the 90% meets one of the 10% the very first thing that happens is that the 90% guy wants to find out every technical detail, about every aspect of the 10% guy's trading strategy, software etc. In doing this, the real essence of WHY the 10% guy is successful is almost always completely missed. This happens in much the same way as we miss huge parts of sales talks and yet we still buy the products.

We almost always default to the comfort path of least resistance. Television advertisers have for years used these methods to make us buy products we don't want or need. The 147 take the time to find out what we WANT to hear, what we WANT to be told. They discover if you like our comfort path and they sell to that path. This comfort path is the main reason why 90% of traders lose money. Just pause for a moment and ask yourself the following question, then consider your inner responses that you pick up on.

Do you think there is a mechanical /computerized/guru system that will continually give you profits? If you do, then ask yourself the following question: What would it mean to you to have this? -Less stress trading? -Better health? -Zero emotions when trading? -More free time? -Self-esteem? -Power? -Material goods? Just play with this for a moment but REALLY focus internally on how the system would be good for you. After you have

THE POWER OF VISUALIZATION AND BELIEF

done this you will have come a long way to discovering part of your comfort path. THIS is the path that you will evaluate any trading product on. THIS is how you will be sold the latest trading idea to come down the pipe. The 10% guy on the other hand does not have a comfortable path for trading; he has something far more reliable. Before we get to that, let's consider the points above and how these will affect your trading. -Let's take 'less stress trading' and see how you could satisfy this. How about: -The latest trading book? -The latest software idea? -A tell me what to do subscription? -A guru's advice? -A trading course to learn new skills? -A gossip forum to pick up tips? Now look back at the list and notice that any one of them will 'help' with the earlier blue text areas. So...the losing 90% are the traders who ultimately believe in the idea that there is an EXTERNAL product/system/concept that will satisfy what they listed under the bulleted points above.

The 10% have no such notion of the above, in fact, they will make money regardless of any product / system / concept they use. The 10% have one thing that every single one of the 90% is looking for. The 90% are not looking at the wrong product, the wrong system or the wrong concept. They are simply looking in the wrong place. IT'S ALL ABOUT WHAT YOU BELIEVE TO BE TRUE RATHER THAT WHAT IS TRUE. What is a belief? What do you believe to be true? It might seem at first like this is an easy question to answer and on the face of it, suppose it is, however once you start to question beliefs, things become not quite so easy to explain. We can say at a simple level that "a belief is something you believe in". But how do measure a belief? Are there different qualities of beliefs? What will these different beliefs mean to 148 you? To gain a better understanding you might try a simple exercise.

1. Think of a belief that you hold that we can validate as being 100% true. You MUST start with a belief something like this: The centre of the sun is hot. 2. Now is the time to think deeply about this belief, best that you close your eyes and focus on this belief. As you focus on this belief become extremely sensitive to how the belief FEELS to you. You need to do this with the utmost commitment to REALLY monitor how this belief is represented to the WHOLE of your very being. (You should

spend about 3-5 minutes on this first part) When finished take a pad and write down every physical feeling or sensory perception that you experienced.
2. Next think of another belief (As this is all about trading we will use the belief that needs to do this with the utmost commitment to REALLY monitoring how this belief is represented to the WHOLE of your very being).
3. You should spend about 3-5 minutes on this second part) When finished take a pad and write down every physical feeling or sensory perception that you experienced to do with this belief.
4. When you have completed steps 1-3 take both beliefs and compare them against EVERYTHING that you felt and experienced. If BOTH beliefs compare the same, i.e. your belief that you are a successful trader produced the same experiences that you felt with the belief that the centre of the sun is hot then you are already one of the 10% who makes vast sums from trading. If you detect differences then you are almost certainly to be one of the 90% I can tell you without doubt that the 10% believe in their ability to make money to the same degree that they believe the sun will rise in the morning. I can further tell you that this is the ONLY difference between the successful and the unsuccessful. Every successful trader I have ever met has an intrinsic belief / knowing that he/she IS successful. On the other hand, every trader I have ever met who is still searching for successful trading is still looking at: The latest all-singing, all-dancing software, The latest and greatest data feed, The latest chart pattern, The very best timeframe, The latest chart indicator (Some software has 1,000's of built-in indicators that all work right! The latest moving average setting, The latest guru's offerings, The latest 'tipster' offering Is daily browsing huge trading forums looking for the 'blind' to lead them to wealth?
5. This list goes on and forever circles within the 90% --End of email document—

I would again like to acknowledge and thank Rakesh for these words of wisdom, which during my trading and investing career I have come to realize are not only accurate but also extremely wise. So belief, when we talk about

VSA, means believing in your system. I have to admit that at the very beginning, as I was learning VSA, I found some of the concepts difficult to grasp. For instance, Tom would say that weakness appears on ultra-high volume up bars, then in the next sentence, he would say that weakness also appears on low-volume up bars. Surely he was contradicting himself. I soon learnt, however, that Tom was completely right and what he was saying was correct.

In summary, our beliefs and what we see around us each day have a profound impact on our existence on this planet. The great Albert Einstein made some very shrewd observations, here are some of his quotes for us to ponder on:

- "Two things are infinite: the universe and human stupidity; and I'm not sure about the universe."
- "There are only two ways to live your life. One is as though nothing is a miracle. The other is as though everything is a miracle."
- "The important thing is not to stop questioning. Curiosity has its own reason for existing. Weakness of attitude becomes weakness of character."

CHAPTER 4
FOOD FOR THOUGHT!

Living Life – Going Down a One-Way Highway – No Going Back!

FOOD FOR THOUGHT!

Living Life – Like Driving a Car / Automobile– Where Are You Looking?

In the rearview mirror – regrets / anger / disappointment / fear / mistakes / broken promises / focus on errors?

Looking out the front, the windscreen – optimistic, creative, control, change, manifestation, happy, positive, in control seeking knowledge?

What Happens When We Drive With Our Main Focus on the Rear View Mirror, Not Looking at What is in Front of us?

We crash!!

Good News Does Not Sell!! We are put in fear by media, social media, chat rooms etc. etc.

FOOD FOR THOUGHT!

FOOD FOR THOUGHT!

The Fact

The Inspiration – Creator's "Find What You Love"

Steve Jobs

Wise words from a genius – Steve Jobs

"You can't connect the dots looking forward; you can only connect them looking backwards. So you have to trust that the dots will somehow connect in your future. You have to trust in something — your gut, destiny, life, karma, whatever. This approach has never let me down, and it has made all the difference in my life".

"I didn't see it then, but it turned out that getting fired from Apple was the best thing that could have ever happened to me. The heaviness of being successful was replaced by the lightness of being a beginner again, less sure about everything. It freed me to enter one of the most creative periods of my life".

"Remembering that I'll be dead soon is the most important tool I've ever encountered to help me make the big choices in life. Because almost everything — all external expectations, all pride, all fear of embarrassment or failure - these things just fall away in the face of death, leaving only what is truly important. Remembering that you are going to die is the best way I know to avoid the trap of thinking you have something to lose. You are already naked. There is no reason not to follow your heart."

Steve Jobs

Live for today and be happy.

How can YOU connect the dots?

FOOD FOR THOUGHT!

Ask yourself these questions?

- Are you in control of your life and circumstances?
- Do you believe you can control your life and circumstances?
- Do you believe you are rich or poor?
- Do you believe you have a direct influence over your current circumstance, good or bad?
- Do you believe in universal laws, either religious or science-based?
- Do you believe you have the power to harness those laws for good or bad?
- Do you want to improve and enhance your life experience?
- ARE YOU WILLING TO USE YOUR MIND LIKE A PARACHUTE – BEST USED WHEN IT IS OPENED?

The POWER OF POSITIVE AFFIRMATION, THINKING AND ACTION IN YOUR LIFE

FOOD FOR THOUGHT!

Can there be anything more important than our thoughts?

Our thoughts create our reality.

The quality of your thinking determines the quality of your life, both personal and professional.

Your thinking can propel you to SUCCESS or it can hold you back!!

FOOD FOR THOUGHT!

DID YOU KNOW?

…We have 60,000 to 80,000 thoughts every day???

FOOD FOR THOUGHT!

…Staggering, isn't it?

…Have you ever wondered WHY you think some thoughts and where they came from??? Why have YOU decided to consciously think about them??

How many of those thoughts do you actively think about and **absorb** which affect the way you feel…Physically and mentally? i.e. Stress, headaches, anxiety, temper, lack of confidence, nausea, worry, pessimism etc.

How many are uplifting, happy and positive thoughts?

How many are negative, worrying, nagging thoughts?

I hear so many people say:

"I can't change because that's the way I am and have always been like that".

"It can't be done"

"I haven't got the confidence"

"I'm terrible at that"

"He / She is better than me at that"

"I'll never get the hang of it"

"He / She has more experience"

These are <u>conditioned</u> thoughts that **CAN BE CHANGED!!...**

…**GREAT NEWS!!**

All you have to do is RECOGNISE when you have started thinking negatively and STOP!

FOOD FOR THOUGHT!

RED LIGHT THAT NEGATIVE THOUGHT and do it FAST!!!!!!

If you keep THINKING negatively you will keep FEELING negative!!!!

The secret to genuinely positive thinking is to RECOGNISE when you are thinking badly. The sooner you RED LIGHT the bad thoughts the sooner YOU WILL FEEL BETTER…

…Can this be done overnight????

No…It will take a little work on your behalf.

If you could pay for a feeling of well-being, confidence, satisfaction, happiness, optimism, HOW MUCH would you pay? I am assuming a great deal.

Really…all you need to do is use the FOUR R's…

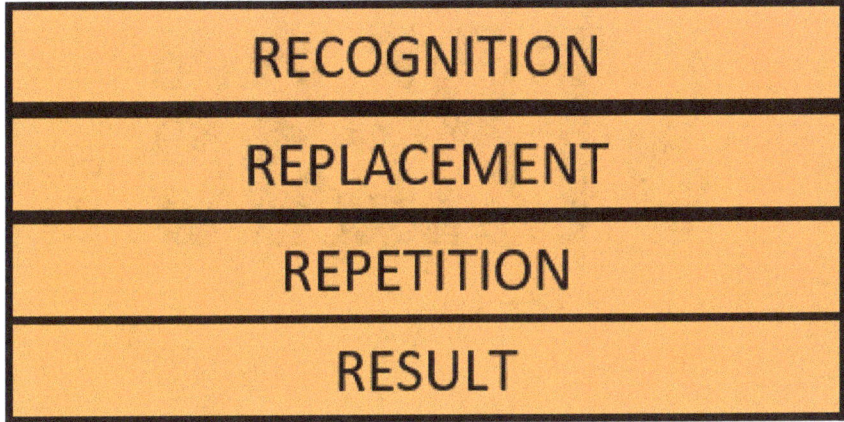

RECOGNISING the negative thoughts when they enter your head.

REPLACING the negative thoughts with positive ones.

REPEAT this until it is second nature.

RESULT will be that the longer you do this the less and less negative thoughts start entering your head and you will FEEL soooooooo much BETTER a whole lot more of the time!!

hmmmmm?...A Word of Warning though…

FOOD FOR THOUGHT!

BEWARE of NEGATIVE ATTITUDES from people who haven't discovered the POWER of POSITIVE THINKING!!! They are treading on THIN ICE and it won't be long before they crash through to the abyss!!!

DO NOT LET THEM TAKE YOU DOWN OR DETER YOU!!!!

So Motivate yourself with your POSITIVE self-talk (the Voice inside your head) and give the NEGATIVE stuff the RED LIGHT.

…and remember…you are not your sub-conscious thoughts and you have limited control over them so go easy on yourself. You only take control when you consciously start absorbing thoughts so DECIDE on which thoughts are good for you and which ones are holding you back!

YOU CAN ALL DO THIS AS IT IS WITHIN ALL OF US SO WHY NOT START…

…RIGHT NOW!!

FOOD FOR THOUGHT!

And finally…

FOOD FOR THOUGHT!

BEWARE of NEGATIVE ATTITUDES from people who haven't discovered the POWER of POSITIVE THINKING!!! They are treading on THIN ICE and it won't be long before they crash through to the abyss!!!

DO NOT LET THEM TAKE YOU DOWN OR DETER YOU!!!!

So Motivate yourself with your POSITIVE self-talk (the Voice inside your head) and give the NEGATIVE stuff the RED LIGHT.

…and remember…you are not your sub-conscious thoughts and you have limited control over them so go easy on yourself. You only take control when you consciously start absorbing thoughts so DECIDE on which thoughts are good for you and which ones are holding you back!

YOU CAN ALL DO THIS AS IT IS WITHIN ALL OF US SO WHY NOT START…

…RIGHT NOW!!

And finally…

A Poem By Walter D Wintle About Thoughts...

If you think you are beaten, you are
If you think you dare not, you don't,
If you like to win, but you think you can't
It is almost certain you won't.
If you think you'll lose, you're lost
For out of the world we find,
Success begins with a fellow's will
It's all in the state of mind.

If you think you are outclassed, you are
You've got to think high to rise,
You've got to be sure of yourself before
You can ever win a prize.

Life's battles don't always go
To the stronger or faster man,
But soon or late the man who wins
Is the man WHO THINKS HE CAN!

Invictus: The Unconquerable

Out of the night that covers me,
Black as the Pit from pole to pole,
I thank whatever gods may be
For my unconquerable soul.

In the fell clutch of circumstance
I have not winced nor cried aloud,
Under the bludgeonings of chance
My head is bloody, but unbowed.

FOOD FOR THOUGHT!

Beyond this place of wrath and tears
Looms but the horror of the shade,
And yet the menace of the years
Finds, and shall find me, unafraid.

It matters not how strait the gate,
How charged with punishments the scroll,
I am the master of my fate:
I am the captain of my soul.

Keep on Smiling & Believing in Yourself, You are a Miracle of this Universe ☺

CHAPTER 5
THOUGHT VIBRATION & ENERGY IN THE MATERIAL WORLD

Energy from the chair where you are sitting, to your thoughts and feelings, energy is all there is. Energy can neither be created nor destroyed. It can only be transformed into a different form of energy. We can only transform and redirect what already is. You see, you are more than just a body living in a physical world. You are made up of energy and exist in a universe where everything is vibrating energy. This means that you have the ability to send and receive energy. In this chapter, we will explore how to harness this powerful force to manifest the reality you desire and use it to your benefit. As Aristotle wisely put it, the energy of the mind is the essence of life. All life vibrates. Everything living moves, all colours and sounds vibrate to a frequency, and nothing sits idle. Many of these frequencies were recorded in ancient Egypt by Hermes.

Some of the designs on ancient structures are actually the patterns of sound vibrations, and when those notes are played, they are music. Some of You will be familiar with 432 Hz. 432 Hz is a **frequency of sound that is used as a tuning standard for music**[12]. It is also known as Verdi's A because it was the preferred pitch of the Italian composer Giuseppe Verdi[1]. Some people believe that 432 Hz is a superior and more natural tuning than the modern standard of 440 Hz and that it has a positive effect on the mind and body. 432 Hz is also an interesting number mathematically, as it is the sum of four consecutive primes and three **grosses.**

Each of these different Hz carries its own unique vibration. Life is vibration, so is mind, so is matter. Electricity, or vibration, is the same energy, same power. You can call it God, Divine Mind, or The Tao, but the Tao that can be named is not the Tao.

All forces are vibration, as all come from one central vibration taking different forms, and as the electrical vibrations are given, know that life itself, to be sure, is the creative force or God, yet its manifestations in man are electrical, or vibratory. Electricity is God in action. Seeing this, feeling this, knowing this, you will find that not only does the body become revivified, but by the creating in every atom of its being the knowledge of the activity of this creative force or principle? As related to spirit, mind, body, all three are renewed. The Buddha said, anything that arises in the mind starts flowing as a sensation in the body. All matter in the universe vibrates at different frequencies, including every living being on Earth. The intensity and frequency of these vibrations are unique to each individual and can vary based on their experiences.

We are attuned to our own vibrations, but they can be influenced by external. Or. Internal forces. Vibrations are a cohesive force in nature, as all forces vibrate at different frequencies, our bodies emit vibrations that control our mental and physical processes which are collectively known as the aura. The aura is a feeling or character that a person or place seems to have. It can also refer to a type of light that some people say they can see around people and animals. The aura is like a bubble of energy that surrounds every living thing. It is an extension of a person's personality and emotional, mental, and physical landscape. The aura can change from day to day and can be affected by external factors.

Each sensory organ in our body reflects a different vibration. According to the teachings of Ascended Masters, Ascended Masters in a number of movements in the theosophical tradition[1] are held to be spiritually enlightened beings who in past incarnations were ordinary humans, but who have undergone a series of spiritual transformations originally called initiations.

Both *mahatma* and *ascended master* are terms used in the Ascended Master Teachings. The concept of an ascended master is based on the theosophical concept of the Mahatma or Masters of the Ancient Wisdom. However, Mahatmas and ascended masters are believed by some to differ in certain respects.

According to the Ascended Master Teachings, a "Master of Light", "Healer" or "Spiritual Master" is a divine human being who has taken the fifth initiation and is thereby capable of dwelling in a fifth dimension. The teachings hold that an "ascended master" is a human being who has taken the sixth Initiation, also referred to as Ascension, and is thereby believed to be capable of dwelling in a sixth dimension.

The term *ascended master* was first used by Baird T. Spalding in 1924 in his series of books, *Life and Teachings of the Masters of the Far East* (DeVorss and Co.), Godfrey Ray King (Guy Ballard) further popularized this concept of spiritual masters who had once lived on the earth in his book *Unveiled Mysteries*.

Raising one's vibration and frequency is the key to transforming any aspect of their life, including the healing of disease. Achieving abundance and attaining transfiguration of the physical body into the ascended realm, he said, I urge you all fervently, I urge you to state, unto the universe, unto the multiverse, I AM. I AM, I AM I AM LIFE. I AM GOD?

I AM as you state the knowingness within your breast, you raise your frequency, the vibration of I AM will begin to pulsate within you. This is because the vibrational frequency of an individual creates a resonance with the energy of the universe, which facilitates the manifestation of their desires and enables them to access higher states of consciousness. By raising one's vibration and frequency, one can align oneself with the universal energy, which in turn helps one to create reality in accordance with their intentions. To comprehend the potential of vibrational energy, it's crucial to recognize the human body as a sophisticated quantum physics apparatus. The human body is composed of nothing but vibrating energy. Cells constitute human beings which are made up of atoms, which are comprised of particles that are essentially probability waves. Most of the physical matter we encounter in our daily lives is actually made up of empty space.

Essentially, we are more vibration than mass, and therefore we can be significantly influenced by vibrational energy. Either positively or negatively, energy is the fundamental force that permeates every aspect of our existence. It is the essence of life, the driving force behind all matter and experiences. To truly tap into our potential and create a fulfilling life, it is essential to understand and harness the power of energy. The role of thoughts in shaping our reality has been a recurring theme in philosophy throughout history. Various philosophers have explored the profound interplay between the mind and the world it perceives.

One perspective assumes that thoughts operate like magnets. Attracting experiences that resonate with their vibrational frequency. Immanuel Kant, a renowned philosopher, did not explicitly discuss the Law of attraction but explored the concept of the mind actively shaping the reality it perceives, he argued that our mental framework, or categories of understanding, serves as a lens through which we interpret and give meaning to our experiences. In this light, our thoughts can be seen as active participants in constructing our lived reality. Eastern philosophy also emphasizes the power of thought in shaping our reality. Lao Su, the ancient Chinese philosopher, suggested that by maintaining a positive and harmonious state of mind, individuals could navigate life's challenges more effectively and attract positive experiences.

By saying to yourself watch your thoughts, they become internal words. Watch your words, for they become actions. Watch your actions, they can become habit. Watch your habits, they become character. What's your character? It becomes your destiny. The practice of cultivating positive thoughts through affirmations, visualization, and gratitude practices can be seen as a proactive step towards creating a more fulfilling and purposeful life. These tools find support in the works of prominent philosophers such as Jean Paul Satra and Aristotle. Such as existentialist philosophy emphasizes individual responsibility and the creation of meaning in a seemingly indifferent universe. Affirmations, which involve consciously choosing positive thoughts and beliefs, resonate with such an idea that we are condemned to be free and exercise our existential freedom.

To shape our subjective experience of reality, basically, like attracts like. If you are vibrating at a certain frequency then you are going to attract people, things and experiences that match that level of vibration. If you want a new car, you have a clear picture of it in your mind, and you take the time to visualize it and feel how it would feel to have that car in your reality, the universe has no other choice but to match you up with that vibration. If you look around you, and all you see are the things that are lacking in your life, that's the level at which you are vibrating and the universe has to match that vibration. We must stay mindful. This is why being aware of ourselves is so important because we are really creating our reality.

Different thoughts, emotions, and feelings possess different vibrational energies or frequencies. The energy of these thoughts, emotions, and feelings often exists in the form of words. Just thinking or speaking a word can emit a certain energy. Once the word is perceived, it is transmuted to the conscious, depending on the word and what type of energy or frequency it generates. The level of vibrational frequency can tell you what level of consciousness the word exists within. Thoughts plus emotions plus feelings equals energy, slash vibrational frequency, e.g. the word love generates a higher vibrational frequency in your consciousness in comparison to the word hate which generates a lower energy frequency. The word peace generates a higher energy frequency than the word worry and speaking the name of God produces one of the highest of energy frequencies, whereas even thinking the name of Satan. Evokes one of the lowest energy frequencies. The notion that emotions and thoughts possess unique vibrations is rooted in the works of ancient philosophers such as Plato. The three parts of the soul are at odds with each other, and it is their struggle that accounts for the variety and complexity of human behaviour. This quote captures Plato's insight into the internal dynamics of the soul, suggesting that reason, spirit and appetite, each with its distinct nature, and desires are in constant interplay. In the current scenario, the correlation between positive emotions and high-frequency vibrations draws parallels with the philosophical musings of existentialists?

Grounded in the belief in the absurdity of existence, encourages individuals to seek significance and happiness in spite of life's inherent uncertainties and challenges.

In the book The myth of Sisyphus by Albert Camus, reflection on the human condition and the tension between the yearning for meaning and the apparent lack of inherent purpose in the universe. In this context, the alliance with positive emotions emanating high-frequency vibrations can be seen as an act of existential rebellion. It is an active decision to imbue life with meaning, positivity, and joy despite the absurdity of existence. Camus urges individuals to embrace their human capacity for creation and to assert their existence happily in the face of the existential void.

On the other hand, the link between negative emotions and low-frequency vibrations resonates with stoicism. An ancient philosophical school of thought, and particularly the teachings of Seneca, stoicism emphasizes the significance of reason, virtue, and inner tranquillity in navigating life's challenges. Seneca, an influential Stoic philosopher, advocated for the mastery of emotions and the cultivation of inner peace regardless of external circumstances. The correlation with negative emotions emanating low-frequency vibrations can be viewed through the Stoic prism as disturbances to the tranquillity that one should strive to maintain. Seneca's writings, such as his letters to Lucilius, underscore the stoic commitment to emotional resilience, urging individuals to confront adversities with a calm and rational mind. By drawing parallels between modern insights into vibrational frequencies and the philosophical perspectives of Cameo and Seneca, a holistic understanding emerges. It highlights the profound interplay between our emotional states and our philosophical orientation toward life. In embracing positive emotions, individuals engage in a rebellion against the absurdity. Infusing their existence with purpose and joy on the Stoic front, the call to master negative emotions aligns with Seneca's emphasis on maintaining inner tranquillity.

Irrespective of external circumstances, in essence, this exploration demonstrates how philosophical perspectives from different eras converge with contemporary notions. Offering a comprehensive framework for understanding the intricate relationship between emotions, vibrations, and our approach to the complexities of human existence, David Bone, a renowned quantum physicist, proposed a theory called the implicate order, which presents an intriguing parallel to the idea of vibrational, frequencies influencing reality according to Bone. Reality is interconnected and unfolds, with visible aspects merely being manifestations of underlying unseen orders.

He suggested that the concept of order is somewhat arbitrary, and there is always a higher degree of order that can be attained. Bones work provides a fascinating insight into the fundamental nature of our universe and its interconnectedness, which has significant implications for our understanding of reality. Throughout history, the powerful link between the mind and body has been acknowledged, with physical well-being playing a significant role in unlocking higher vibrations. And optimizing overall existence. This holistic approach recognizes the interdependence of mental and physical states, and by prioritizing physical health, one can pave the way for an elevated state of being. In order to achieve optimal physical function and sustained energy and vitality, a balanced and nourishing diet forms another crucial element in the pursuit of higher vibrations. It is essential to view nutritional intake not as a mere routine but as a conscious choice that impacts the body's energy levels. Whole, nutrient-dense foods provide the essential building blocks for promoting overall well-being.

In summary, prioritizing physical health through regular exercise and a balanced, nourishing diet can help achieve an elevated state of being and unlock higher. Vibrations. Maintaining high vibrational energy levels is crucial for optimal physical and mental function. Adequate rest and relaxation play a vital role in achieving this state. Sleep is the body's natural healer, and a cornerstone of this principle, since it is during this time that the body repairs and rejuvenates itself, incorporating mindfulness practices, hobbies, or spending time in nature in daily life becomes an intentional act of self-care that promotes relaxation. The core premise of these practices is that optimal health allows energy to flow freely through the body aligning with the eastern concept of key, or prana, the life force that courses through the body.

When energy flows unimpeded individuals can tap into their full potential both mentally and physically. A visual metaphor for this state is that of a river flowing smoothly, unobstructed by debris. In this state, individuals are more resilient, adaptable and better positioned to navigate the currents of life, therefore incorporating rest and relaxation into daily routines is essential for a well-lived life and maximizing one's potential. The perspective of engaging viewers involves encouraging them to view their well-being as an integrated approach to harmony. Using mind and body instead of a series of isolated habits, this perspective acknowledges that the pursuit of higher vibrations is a holistic journey, which should be woven into the fabric of daily life. By consciously making choices in exercise, nutrition, and rest, viewers are not only investing in their physical health but also raising the overall frequency of their existence.

This holistic approach is a call to action, resonating with the understanding that our bodies are not just vessels, but dynamic components in the symphony of a vibrantly lived. Life. The human body is capable of producing and emitting various frequencies of energy, which collectively determine an individual's overall vibrational frequency. To elevate this frequency, there are several accessible tools and resources available. One such tool is meditation, an ancient practice that enables individuals to quiet the mind and create a serene mental space. By reducing stress and fostering a connection with the inner self, meditation becomes a gateway to tapping into the boundless well of energy residing within each of us. Another way to raise vibrational frequency is through energy healing modalities like rekey, acupuncture and sound healing. These modalities recognize the subtle energies that course through our bodies and offer techniques to clear blockages, restore balance to energy centers and elevate our vibrational frequency.

Affirmations and visualization become powerful tools for reprogramming the subconscious mind. These tools harness the power of the mind to create positive changes in an individual's vibrational frequency. The use of these tools can help a person embark on a journey of self-discovery and revitalization, tapping into the innate ability of the body to restore. Or harmony and equilibrium, the practice of positive affirmations helps individuals align their beliefs with their intentions. By visualizing desired outcomes individuals can further enhance this process creating a fertile ground for positive transformation in their subconscious.

Another effective way to raise one's vibrations is through nature connection, which allows individuals to absorb the high vibrations inherent in the natural world. This immersive experience can be achieved through activities such as hiking, strolling in a park, or simply finding solace under a tree. These tools are versatile resources, adaptable to individual preferences and lifestyles. The key lies in actively engaging with them and weaving them into the fabric of daily life. By doing so, individuals can embark on a journey of raising vibrations and experience a more vibrant and harmonious existence with the support and guidance of these steadfast companions.

The concept of raising your vibration is not just a one-time practice, it is a way of life. By embracing the power of energy in our daily lives, we can unlock our full potential. And create a reality that aligns with our highest aspirations. To harness the power of energy in your daily life, you can follow some simple yet effective steps. Firstly, practicing gratitude cultivates an attitude of gratitude, which raises our vibrations and attracts more things to be grateful for. Secondly, mindful living is crucial as being present in the moment and fully engaged in whatever you're doing. Lastly, surrounding yourself with positive energy is essential. Surround yourself with people, places, and things that uplift and inspire you. Engage in activities that bring you joy and make you feel alive. By following these steps, you can significantly improve your life quality and overall well-being.

CHAPTER 6
THE POWER OF WORDS, THE INNER VOICE, AND EMOTIONAL RESPONSES

Think of the words of Mahatma Gandhi and Martin Luther King that inspired millions to seek freedom. Words are not just sounds, they are powerful tools that can inspire. Heal and transform Science backs this up. Think of the words of Mahatma Gandhi and Martin Luther King that inspired millions to seek freedom. Research shows that words can affect our brains, feelings and even, our health. Positive words can improve our mood and immune system, while negative words can cause stress and sickness. But it's not just about what we say, to others. The words we speak to ourselves matter just as much, if not more. Self-talk shapes our beliefs and actions, often without us even realizing it. Now let's take this a step further, what if the words we use could communicate with the universe itself? This idea is, central to, the Law of Attraction. The belief is that our thoughts and words can bring us what we want.

The Law of Attraction says that the energy from our thoughts and words sends out vibrations that the universe reacts to. Positive, focused words can bring good results. While negative words can cause bad outcomes, so how do we talk to the universe effectively? It starts with choosing the right, words, Here are some practical tips to get you started. First, focus on positive affirmations, phrases like, I am capable, I am deserving of success. And I attract abundance. Can shift your mindset and energy. Write them down, say them out loud and repeat them daily.

Next, use visualization techniques. When you visualize your goals, describe them in detail as if they are already happening. This reinforces the message to the universe and strengthens your belief in your ability to achieve them. Integrate these practices into your daily routine. Whether it's during meditation, before bed, or while journaling, make time to speak your intentions, clearly, and, positively. Many people have harnessed the power of words to transform their lives. Oprah Winfrey, for instance, has often spoken about the importance of positive affirmations in her journey to success.

Everyday individuals have stories to share, from overcoming illness to achieving career goals, the power of words has been a guiding force in their journeys. However, it's easy to fall into the trap of negative self-talk, words like, I can't, I'm not good enough or this will never work can sabotage our efforts. Recognizing and correcting these patterns is crucial. Start by identifying your limiting beliefs and challenge them with positive empowering statements. Shift your language from I can't to I can and watch how your reality begins to change.

In summary, the words we choose can, shape, our, reality, in, profound, ways, By speaking positively and intentionally, we can align ourselves with the universe and attract the life we desire. Thank you for joining us on, this, journey, at, mind, matrix, We encourage you to practice the power of words daily and witness the incredible transformations that follow. Remember, the? Universe, is? Always, listening?

Speak wisely and Live abundantly.

Remember, stay empowered and keep exploring the boundless potential within you.

At times, you are going to fail, and you are going to fail, and you are going fail again, and then you're going to win. And that's life. Listen to the many athletes at this year's 2024 Olympics in Paris as I write this and they all tell similar stories of the mountains they had to climb, the hurdles they had to jump, the pain and suffering of training every day, seven days a week to become the best.

THE POWER OF WORDS, THE INNER VOICE, AND EMOTIONAL RESPONSES

They get to the Olympics and some come last in their chosen skill. But many come back four years later and are on the podium. They are not superhuman, they have belief and take massive action to get better, and often this works.

Life without those challenges is just existence. Don't just exist. Go and live.

Inaction, procrastination, self-doubt, depression will cost you, but your default setting should be, I am going to do something, just get up, and move towards that challenge. And go and attack it. Go and do something that's hard. Struggle hurts but it depends on how you frame it. If you want freedom in your life, you have to have discipline. Move towards that challenge, whatever that challenge is, and you may be successful and you may not be successful, but you will be better. And the next challenge, you will be more prepared for.

We are going to have wins, we're going to have losses, we are going to have great results and we are going to have poor results. We are going to have good nights, we're going to have bad nights, we're going to have good relationships, we are going to have bad relationships, we are going to have good ideas and bad ideas, we are going to make money, we're going lose money, all these things are going to happen at some point, it's unavoidable and part of being human.

And if you oscillate emotionally up and down drastically, it's going to be problematic.

I know, when I was a serving police officer with Hampshire and the Metropolitan Police I saw some awful things and ended up with PTSD. I got help and then reframed my outlook, accepting that being a Police Officer will often put you in a position to see the worst in society when in fact most people will never encounter what I saw in an entire lifetime.

Embrace those emotions, but don't let those emotions embrace you. Keep pushing through things that are not working out the way you would want or expect. This is a very difficult thing to do because it hurts. Say to yourself I'm going forward; I am not going to quit. As the great Bear Grylls states many times on his shows, and indeed where he writes his books on his Ireland of the coast of Wales, he has a log cabin where he focuses and writes and above the entrance is a placard, it says.

Never Give Up!

If you find yourself in an unpleasant situation and it's your fault take ownership of it, and I'm fix it. That's what extreme ownership is, because when you look around at your life and you look around at your job and your financial situation, and your relationships, and your physical health when you look at all those things, and all the problems that you may have with those things, are you the reason you have all those problems and it is because of you. That can hurt. That can stay. And a lot of times, our ego rejects that and makes excuses and lies, and then we don't have to change anything and then nothing changes. When the excuses all go away and people can actually confront the fact that this is all because of me it hurts. But it is also unbelievably empowering, because the more discipline you have in your life, the more freedom you will end up with. So, if you lack the discipline to exercise and eat healthy, you'll end up being a slave to disease.

If you lack the discipline to work hard, save and manage your money effectively, you will end up a slave to finances if you lack the discipline to manage your time and finances correctly. You will end up with no free time if you have no self-discipline. If you have the discipline to save your money and work hard, invest your money wisely and if you have the discipline to manage your time correctly and not waste a bunch of time everything just falls into place.

If you have the discipline to exercise and eat healthy, drink healthy and yes I mean no alcohol (I was a heavy drinker for years but one day woke up and said enough is enough and I have never touched an alcoholic beverage since) you will end up with total freedom. And you're going to start to progress in every aspect of your life. And you'll see that if you have that kind of discipline right now, you are going to end up with freedom and power. You will attain freedom.

You're not shackled, the universe we are part of wants you to succeed and be happy. The universe loves speed, and all the answers you need for a purpose-driven and fulfilling life are speeding their way to you right now. You need not strive about this, you need not worry about this, just believe and your faith will make it so.

So if you're in the woods and you don't know where to go, start walking. You have got to start walking because the perspective is not going to change. You have to start moving forward. But standing there lost and not doing anything is just waiting to die, waiting to starve to death. Don't let that happen. It's really important because as humans, we don't, want to get conflicting messages about our emotions and how to express them and what that looks like.

There's a lot of men and women struggling right now. Letting my emotions run my life is letting them control me and not vice versa. Human faith is everything so don't let negativity get into your psyche. It's really important because we get conflicting messages about emotion and how to express this in today's fast-paced world with social media bullying rife and pressure to succeed at every level. There's a lot of men and women struggling right now, every human faces challenges, and you know what they've been through. Suppressing the feelings of despair or guilt isn't going to help, and nor is letting them run your life because you're sad now you're going to make a bunch of bad decisions because you said, no, no, it doesn't, doesn't work like that. It just doesn't work like that. You're sad, okay? You get emotional sometimes, okay? Got it. Now get control of your emotions. And carry on with your life, and sometimes you're going to get hit with a baseball bat. And that's okay, oh I am having an emotional moment right now, there's something wrong with me!!

No, there's nothing wrong with you, there's nothing wrong with you at all. The other extreme is, oh, am letting my emotions run my life and I'm making a bunch of bad decisions and you list excuses in your mind which will respond as you ask of it. Tell it to feel depressed, it will obey. Tell it to feel guilt, it will obey, tell it life is miserable and the world is a terrible place with wars, riots, mass shootings and despair and that's what your mind will see more of.

Guess what? It's time to carry on and see the world and its beauty. Albert Einstein said in his essay "How I see the World" and I quote:

"How strange is the lot of us mortals! Each of us is here for a brief sojourn; for what purpose he knows not, though he sometimes thinks he senses it. But without deeper reflection, one knows from daily life that one exists for other people -- first of all for those upon whose smiles and well-being our own happiness is wholly dependent, and then for the many, unknown to us, to whose destinies we are bound by the ties of sympathy. A hundred times every day I remind myself that my inner and outer life are based on the labours of other men, living and dead and that I must exert myself in order to give in the same measure as I have received and am still receiving...

"I have never looked upon ease and happiness as ends in themselves -- this critical basis I call the ideal of a pigsty. The ideals that have lighted my way, and time after time have given me new courage to face life cheerfully, have been Kindness, Beauty, and Truth. Without the sense of kinship with men of like mind, without the occupation with the objective world, the eternally unattainable in the field of art and scientific endeavours, life would have seemed empty to me. The trite objects of human efforts -- possessions, outward success, luxury -- have always seemed to me contemptible.

"My passionate sense of social justice and social responsibility has always contrasted oddly with my pronounced lack of need for direct contact with other human beings and human communities. I am truly a 'lone traveller' and have never belonged to my country, my home, my friends, or even my immediate family, with my whole heart; in the face of all these ties, I have never lost a sense of distance and a need for solitude..."

"My political ideal is democracy. Let every man be respected as an individual and no man idolized. It is an irony of fate that I myself have been the recipient of excessive admiration and reverence from my fellow beings, through no fault, and no merit, of my own. The cause of this may well be the desire, unattainable for many, to understand the few ideas to which I have with my feeble powers attained through ceaseless struggle. I am quite aware that for any organization to reach its goals, one man must do the thinking and directing and generally bear the responsibility. But the led must not be coerced, they must be able to choose their leader. In my opinion, an autocratic system of coercion soon degenerates; force attracts men of low morality... The really valuable thing in the pageant of human life seems to me not the political state, but the creative, sentient individual, the personality; it alone creates the noble and the sublime, while the herd as such remains dull in thought and dull in feeling.

"This topic brings me to that worst outcrop of herd life, the military system, which I abhor... This plague-spot of civilization ought to be abolished with all possible speed. Heroism on command, senseless violence, and all the loathsome nonsense that goes by the name of patriotism -- how passionately I hate them!

"The most beautiful experience we can have is the mysterious. It is the fundamental emotion that stands at the cradle of true art and true science. Whoever does not know it and can no longer wonder, no longer marvel, is as good as dead, and his eyes are dimmed. It was the experience of mystery -- even if mixed with fear -- that engendered religion. A knowledge of the existence of something we cannot penetrate, our perceptions of the profoundest reason and the most radiant beauty, which only in their most primitive forms are accessible to our minds: it is this knowledge and this emotion that constitute true religiosity. In this sense, and only this sense, I am a deeply religious man... I am satisfied with the mystery of life's eternity and with a knowledge, a sense, of the marvellous structure of existence -- as well as the humble attempt to understand even a tiny portion of the Reason that manifests itself in nature."

Remember, don't do well, you are in control. It is your wonderful life. If you are in the problem, you won't see the solution to the problem. Take a step back and detach from the chaos. Detach from the male, detach from your emotions, detach from your ego and be able to assess the best way to execute. That is the job of a leader. If you take any trait of a human being and you take it to an extreme, masculine or feminine, or otherwise you take it to an extreme it's, it's going to. Be, a? problem. Is it good to have no emotions whatsoever? No. That's called a sociopath. Is it good to let your emotions run your life and make your decisions based on your emotions, no, that's not good either? What do we wanna be a, as a human, as a man, when we are balanced? It's much it's much easier to be extreme it's it's it's much easier to say oh no emotions cool and turn them off. That's easier. Or, a total emotional mayhem, that's easier, it's harder to find balance. It's harder to find balance in business, hard to find balance, life is hard to find balance, but you have to be balanced. Because what I want is for the team to win. So be balanced. You're going to be okay because love is the driving force of nature and the universe of which you are an integral part, if only you have faith, belief and knowledge that we are all one, connected through energy.

I end this chapter with the lyrics to one of my favorite songs by the artist Black. This is very poignant as I write this as I recently lost a good friend, Will Myers, at age 53. He leaves a wife and three children and they played this at his funeral. It made me realize they when our time is up we go. Live each day as though it could be your last, for someday it surely will. Life is precious, enjoy it and be positive, kind, and caring of others and you will see immediate changes if you are currently feeling low. I have been there more than once, at one stage contemplating taking my own life. What an idiot I was but thanks to the grace of God I am here with a wife and three wonderful kids enjoying every moment.

A Wonderful Life by Black

Here I go out to sea again
The sunshine fills my hair
And dreams hang in the air
Gulls in the sky and in my blue eye
You know it feels unfair
There's magic everywhere
Look at me standing
Here on my own again
Up straight in the sunshine

THE POWER OF WORDS, THE INNER VOICE, AND EMOTIONAL RESPONSES

No need to run and hide
It's a wonderful, wonderful life
No need to laugh and cry
It's a wonderful, wonderful life

Sun's in your eyes, the heat is in your hair
They seem to hate you
Because you're there
And I need a friend, oh, I need a friend
To make me happy
Not stand here on my own
Look at me standing
Here on my own again
Up straight in the sunshine

No need to run and hide
It's a wonderful, wonderful life
No need to laugh and cry
It's a wonderful, wonderful life
I need a friend, oh, I need friend
To make me happy
Not so alone
Look at me here
Here on my own again
Up straight in the sunshine
No need to run and hide
It's a wonderful, wonderful life

No need to hide and cry
It's a wonderful, wonderful life
No need to run and hide
It's a wonderful, wonderful life
No need to run and hide
It's a wonderful, wonderful life
A wonderful life, It's a wonderful life.

The Power of the Subconscious Mind And Its Influence On Your Life And Actions

The subconscious mind is the part of the mind that is not in the state of awareness. This part of mind contains the memory banks, thought generators, emotions generators, a sensory input controller, and a dedicated storage for habits.

The subconscious mind is basically responsible for recording events gathered through five sensory organs, producing thoughts or emotions, and providing habits or autopilot programs to the conscious mind.

Parts of the Subconscious Mind

Subconscious mind has the following five basic parts:

Memory

This is the place where all the information you gathered through your sensory organs and thoughts generated from realizations/emotions are stored.

The memory bank can remember information when it is **extreme emotion, divergent information, relational information,** and through **repeated actions** or rehearsal.

Among the four ways of remembering, extreme emotions and divergent information get remembered easily by the mind. Because of the involvement of the mind-body in extreme emotion or divergent information, which leads to deep attention and visualization, you remember easily.

You may remember only a few childhood incidents; try to recall what you remember from your childhood. I hope all of the incidents involve certain kind of extreme emotion, whether it may of happiness, sadness, nervousness, or excitement.

Remembering through relational information is quite easier than remembering through rehearsal. For example, you know the spelling of 'nation' and 'ass'. If we relate these two words to remember the spelling of assassination=ass+ass+i+nation, I think it would be easier to remember.

The rehearsal, the time-consuming way of remembering, I think I don't need to explain to you, you know it well.

Autopilot Storage

Autopilot programs are developed through repeated actions or rehearsal. Autopilots are also called habits, it may be good or bad. Only the conscious mind can discriminate between good or bad habits, for the subconscious mind, habits are just habits; there are no good or bad habits.

You might not be able to read Chinese, but you can read English. You have trained your mind to recognize English letters, then recognize words, and then sentences over a period of time. That's how you developed the habit of reading English through rehearsal.

The default life-controlling programs are also autopilot programs. These are mapped to the conscious mind for some time to run your consciousness knowingly or unknowingly.

In the journey of life skill development to make yourself conscious intelligent, you have to erase the corrupted default programs of your subconscious mind by doing the following tasks:

Task One: Identify corrupted default programs

Task Two: Develop a filter program to reject those corrupted programs

Task Three: Replace whatever necessary

Sensory Input Controller

In high school, you have studied the five sensory organs responsible for making our experiences with the outer world.

The sensory input controller is responsible for the following four basic tasks with the five sensory inputs;

1. Sending sensory information to the memory bank

2. Polling sensory inputs when you are engaged state of mind
3. Providing feedback for thought generation
4. Providing feedback for feeling generation
5. The sensory information can be of image, sound, sensation, smell. Out of these four types of inputs that you gather through five sensory organs, you can think only in the form of images and sound, nobody can think of sensation or smell, it can be felt in real-time.

Thought Generator

Thought can be structured or unstructured. When you think knowingly it is called structured thinking, and when unknowingly, it is unstructured.

The thought generator takes information from the memory bank and sensory input controller with the help of autopilot storage to produce and resultant thought.

Memory Bank

As I mentioned already, it is a real-time phenomenon that takes input from the sensory organs to produce feelings. Sometimes feelings are combined with thoughts to produce a mixture out of it.

The basic functions of the subconscious mind are:

- Recording Events
- Producing thoughts or emotions
- Controlling habits

Recording Events

Subconscious mind is always in recording mode. Whatever gets your attention, the subconscious mind puts the information into its memory bank. However, everything recorded in the subconscious mind can't be remembered for long.

I have already mentioned that the subconscious mind can remember extreme emotions and divergent information easily. In the state of extreme emotion and getting divergent information through sensors, you let many parts of your mind & body engage, and that inclusiveness lets the subconscious mind remember easily.

The subconscious mind also remembers through rehearsal or repeated actions. Human memory is like the capacitive memory of a digital computer. When you repeat something for long, you refresh the circuits for that particular information and get remembered.

In remembering relational information for a long period, the subconscious mind refreshes the memory cells of the related information and it becomes easier to remember.

Producing Thoughts or Emotions

Thoughts or emotions are produced through combinations and permutations of the memories within the subconscious. The subconscious mind produces thoughts and emotions in response to events. Events may be of external sensory inputs or your psychological state.

Suppose, you have already memorized the thought "fear of dogs" in subconscious mind. Whenever you see a dog through the sensory eye, your thought "fear of dogs" evokes, it passes the boundary of the conscious mind and loads into the processing unit. When the thought loads into the processing unit, the processing unit asks the subconscious mind to return the emotion of fear to it, and you experience fear.

Controlling Habits

Through repetition, you have developed many habits in your life. The habits are passed to the processing unit without much intervention of the [conscious mind](). Habits run on autopilot within your mind.

Suppose, when you drive a car, you don't need to tell the leg to push the brake whenever required. Similarly, we can read English letters & words without much intervention in pattern recognition.

The subconscious mind has unlimited storage. Habits are the most effective tool to unfold the power of the subconscious mind.

Did you know, "Successful people have a habit to make habits"?

However, your intelligence depends upon what you provide & practice throughout life. If you practice distraction & provide unwanted thoughts to the subconscious mind willingly or unwillingly; you may live a life full of distraction.

What Is Consciousness? 3 States and 5 Functions Of The Conscious Mind

The human mind has basically three parts: conscious mind, subconscious mind, and the processing unit. Consciousness is the state of the conscious mind. Although it is hard to define consciousness, basically consciousness evolves through practice and works as a gateway to the processing unit of our brain.

When we sleep, our processing unit of the brain takes rest, but the consciousness doesn't. The sensory inputs are directly fed into the subconscious mind when any sensation passes the boundary of consciousness, you might get awakened during sleep.

Depending upon the knowing or unknowing mental diets and practices throughout life, we all experience different levels of consciousness at different times. Basically, we have three levels of consciousness.

Consciousness can be reflecting, analytical, or transcendental. Reflection is the most basic level of consciousness and transcendental consciousness is the supreme level of consciousness.

We all experience all these states of consciousness throughout life, however, for most of the people on this planet, transcendental consciousness sparks for a while, instead of illuminating the intelligence. This life skills development series is designed for anyone to illuminate the intelligence, in the meanwhile let's get acquainted with the three states of consciousness in detail.

Reflecting Consciousness

Animals live in this state of consciousness. Whatever enters the subconscious mind through sensors gets passed through the gateway of consciousness without any kind of analysis or comprehension and loads into the processing unit of the brain.

While an owner of a dog goes for a walk with his untrained dog, you might have observed that the dog pulls the owner here and there. Whatever catches the dog's attention, the dog gets attracted to it. However, if the dog is trained to handle distraction through commands, the owner might be able to keep the dog focused on the walk.

In the case of humans, sensory inputs and memorized information or thoughts may pass the boundary of consciousness and get loaded into the processing unit without filtration or analysis. When humans live in this state of consciousness, people often get fooled.

Suppose a WhatsApp message "Abraham Lincoln was really a Vampire Hunter" has been circulated to a group of ignorant people frequently for a month. One person of the group strongly rejected the message and got angry by seeing this message, because he identifies himself as a fan of Abraham Lincoln. Most of the people in that group memorized the WhatsApp message unknowingly by repeatedly seeing it. Their consciousness can't decide as they let anything pass through the boundary of the conscious mind. After a year, another intelligent gentleman asked one of them "Is it true that Abraham Lincoln was a Vampire Hunter?" Then one of the ignorant people reflected on his memorized information unknowingly and said, "Yes it is true, I have read the news in many newspapers." He was firm in his view; it was hard for the gentleman to convince him that it was fake news.

Analytical Consciousness

In this level, people don't let anything pass the boundary of consciousness easily as happens in the reflecting consciousness level. When the mind is trained to reach this level of consciousness, the program of consciousness decides what to pass and what not to pass to the processing unit.

If a person has attention disorder (happens due to unknowing practices), he might not be able to always keep his mind in the analytical state of consciousness. However, if the person becomes self-aware, he may recognize when he becomes reflecting conscious.

Consider the example of WhatsApp fake news: "Abraham Lincoln was really a vampire hunter". When the message gets the attention of a person of analytical consciousness level for the first time, the person may discard it as fake. However, if the message frequently gets his attention many times, the probability of getting memorized unknowingly is 50/50. After one year, if the intelligent gentleman again asks the analytical conscious person the same question, "Is it true that Abraham Lincoln was a vampire hunter?" the person might get confused. Because, he is reflecting on the memorized fake information but, his analytical mind doesn't accept it.

Transcendental Consciousness

This is the ultimate level of consciousness when a person becomes attentive, aware, and intelligent enough to filter out and differentiate all the information and thoughts seeking to load into the processing unit of the mind all the time.

Creative thinking, critical thinking, hypothetical thinking, and metacognition work at their best at this level of consciousness. Through intense devotion towards mindfulness, anyone can reach this level through practice. In this state, the mind can be trained to run Intelligence skills on autopilot, in which intelligence becomes intuition to reach the ultimate stage of life skills development- conscious intelligence.

Let me explain this state of consciousness through an example.

Suppose, in the ecology class of the high school, we all have studied the food cycle. The food cycle essentially tells us the interdependence of the species of nature. We all are living on this planet because of the natural conditions we have. If someone is sent to Mars without the necessary tools, he wouldn't survive there. So, essentially care for the physical self is the care for nature, we are all interdependent in this nature. Transcendental consciousness is when through self-introspection one identifies himself with the cosmos because it is the very basic way of our existence. If someone believes in the identity of cosmos, it is again the reflecting consciousness.

If the fake news "Abraham Lincoln was really a vampire hunter" is sent to a person living in the transcendental consciousness. The person will analyse its authenticity & recognize it as a fake and he will never get confused with it. Because he is always attentive, he will always remember it as fake news.

Five Functions of Consciousness

Basically, consciousness has five distinct functions; we all exhibit these functions exclusively or inclusively depending upon a particular moment. The functions of consciousness are:

Reflection

As the name reflection suggests, it is a state where thoughts, information, and emotions from the subconscious are directly loaded into the processing unit without much filtration and analysis by the conscious mind.

Suppose, a boy named Peter was attracted to a girl named Julie. Whenever he saw that girl; his thought of attraction loads into the processing unit of the brain directly passing the consciousness without analysis. His thought of attraction may be due to physical attraction, emotional attraction, or psychological attraction. Within a month of this happening, they fall into the so-called love. However, their relationship ended after a period of one year. Peter had a desire to marry her but, the desire was unfulfilled. That unfulfilled desire made him angry and now, he is facing anxiety attack. The anxiety is nothing but a thought that was built over time in his subconscious mind. Now, whenever the thought of anxiety is evoked, his reflecting consciousness can't filter out the thoughts and let the processing unit load it.

As a consequence of this, he feels anxiety.

Filtration

This function of the subconscious mind discards certain subconscious output such as thoughts, emotions, and sensory inputs for a particular moment.

Suppose, you were engaged in watching an interesting documentary, in the meanwhile, your mom asked you to come outside. You heard her but couldn't listen to her. So you didn't respond to her and were busy watching the documentary as nobody called you. In this case, your consciousness filtered the voice not to reach fully at the processing unit and as a result, you didn't respond to her.

When you master the art of filtration by the conscious mind for the right purpose, you may eventually discard unwanted thoughts, unwanted conversations, and much more.

Differentiation

In the function of differentiation, your conscious mind works in the feedback mode with the subconscious mind and the processing unit.

The conscious mind takes information from the subconscious and lets it process in the processor. Depending upon the result from the processor, the conscious mind asks for more related information from the subconscious if required.

For example, you are documenting an HR policy for your organization. You have to put the terms & conditions for punishment for illegal activities by employees. In this case, you will encounter "What-If" analysis. Suppose, the processing unit asks you to find the result "If an employee engages in cybercrime." Your consciousness will ask the subconscious what is the solution, if the subconscious has a solution it will provide otherwise the subconscious will tell the conscious, "Google it."

Imaginations

Manifesting the subconscious information or thoughts into reality or into the reality of another dimension is the act of imagination by the conscious mind.

Imagination is a reality for the conscious mind. It is the individual's imagination and the individual's reality. For another person, the imagination of another person might be merely a fiction.

For example, when a creative writer writes a script for a cinema, the story of the cinema becomes reality in the imagination of the writer and that lets the writer present the cinema elegantly. For the viewers, the script is a fictional story but, if the writer is good at his imagination, the writer may be able to let the viewers feel the cinema as reality while watching.

Involvement of the processing unit of the mind creates a distinction between imagination & dreaming. While dreaming, your conscious mind and the subconscious mind work similarly to the actions of imagination, but, your processing unit does not function fully to make the dream a fully functional reality.

Transcendence

When the consciousness becomes attentive, aware, and conscious all the time to [run intelligence skills on autopilot](); the mind functions in the transcendence.

Your transcendental consciousness might be able to spark the bulb of your mind, through attentive practices; you can illuminate the bulb of your mind.

In this function, the conscious mind lets differentiation, filtration, and reflection run on autopilot while the consciousness is awake to determine the individual's right way of doing.

The conscious mind lets the intuition overtake its function although consciousness is fully aware of its functionalities.

Creative thinking is one of the states of transcendence.

Are you creative? Yes, you are creative; we all humans are creative to a certain extent. It doesn't matter the impact of creativity, how big or small it is. The only thing that matters is the transcendental experience of creativity. Everything happens so perfectly and quickly when you encounter creative ideas. Try to recall your experiences.

We all are learning all the time, wherever we give our attention, it gets remembered. It is important to know how to be attentive in the right direction to control your mind and live in a state of transcendental consciousness.

In the journey of life skill development, I think you and everyone will thrive to live in the transcendental state of consciousness. Do you want to live in the transcendence state of spark for a while or illuminate your mind all the time? Do let me know in the comment

"Intelligence skills run on autopilot" means that the intelligence becomes so sharp that intelligence becomes intuition. There are certain basic characteristics every conscious intelligent person has, the characteristics are:

Listening: Active Listener

Speaking: Clarity of thoughts while speaking

Problem-Solving: Solves problems through intuition

Self-Awareness: Have awareness of the self and nature

Personal Power: Have the power to make everybody feel empowered

Lifestyle: Simple and energetic

Empathy: Great empathy makes them great leaders.

Decision-Making: Able to make collective decisions through global thinking.

Management: Have the capability to involve the right people at the right time.

Leadership: Have the capability to make leaders of leading leaders.

These are only a few characteristics to mention for a conscious intelligent person.

Most of the people of the renaissances have these qualities. Nowadays, we only encounter a few people of this kind. Everyone can be conscious intelligent, only devotion towards learning is required to become conscious intelligent. Do you want to be conscious intelligent? If yes, stick to the next section.

Four Ways to Be Conscious Intelligent

To become conscious intelligence, you need to have the self-awareness to recognize the significance of attentiveness, learning, and consciousness.

I have divided the ways to become conscious intelligent into four basic steps;

Devotion towards learning

Being attentive towards duty

Making intelligence a habit through rehearsal

Devotion Towards Learning

How can anyone learn if he/she has no interest to learn?

But, in reality, everyone learns, an ignorant also learns every day and the most intelligent person also learns every day.

Your intelligence depends upon how you learn and what you learn. Basically, if you provide mental diets relevant to your life, you are the intelligent one.

We all have 24 hours a day, in the 24 hours' cycle, someone dedicated time and energy to learn physics, and he became a physicist. At the same time, two people dedicated time and energy to watch reality shows (fictional). After a year, one became ignorant and the other one became the director of another reality show.

If you really want to be a conscious intelligent, you have to understand that we all have limited time and energy, if you utilize this time and energy to provide mental diets relevant to your life, you are on the right path, and otherwise, you are wasting your precious time & energy consciously or unconsciously.

You also need to implement the right way of learning for you. Everyone has [different ways of learning](#), what is your way of learning? Do let me know in the comments.

Being Attentive Towards Duty

What would happen if you start thinking of something else while doing your duty?

Being conscious means you are aware and focused on your work. Suppose, you own a business and reading the book "How to Restructure Your Business". If you start thinking about restructuring your business while reading, you might fail to understand the essence of the book. And, after reading the book, you are making the restructuring plan of your business; you are also planning the risk management for the business. But, what would happen if you become sad or happy while making the risk plan?

When your attention from your duty wanders away, you have to practice bringing it back, that's how you can train your mind to be focused on your duty.

Making Intelligence a Habit Through Rehearsal

When you went to primary school, you were taught to recognize English letters, then English words, and then English sentences. Now you read word by word to understand the English language.

Suppose you are asked to read Chinese, can you read? If you are not familiar with Chinese, you can't even recognize a single letter. But, through repetition, you have trained your mind to read English intuitively.

Similarly, through repetition, you can intuitively calculate $1+1=2$; someone might intuitively calculate $1005+19000$. The intuitive calculation also depends upon practice.

Your all intelligence skills can also run intuitively if you practice them for a long period of time just like calculating mathematical problems intuitively. As you are reading this article, I think you have the intelligence to analyse each and every line intuitively; you don't need to tell your mind to analyse it. Similarly, you can make habits of running all intelligence skills intuitively through rehearsal.

Becoming Aware of the Self

In its basic structure, the self consists of the mind & the physical body.

In another article, I have explained self-awareness in detail.

The mind has three basic parts, primary processing unit, the gateway programs or the conscious mind, and the subconscious mind. Whatever passes through the gateway of consciousness, the primary processing unit picks it and processes, and we experience the reflection of it.

In the journey of becoming conscious intelligent, you have to make the gateway strong, so that unnecessary thoughts or desires can't pass the gateway.

Another part of the self is the physical body, which basically lives on oxygen and food. Oxygen and food are products of nature, every tiny organism and gigantic tree have contributed to providing our physical diets.

Essentially, self-awareness is the art of having cognizance of the mind and the physical nature, through which the driver of life is able to continue the journey of life.

Apart from becoming attentive, self-aware, and conscious; you also need to master the art of controlling unwanted thoughts, anxiety and depression. Become the controller of your mind as well.

Pay attention to whatever you do will be the most essential skill to become conscious intelligence.

Some Words of Wisdom from Dr. Wayne Dyer Who Has Been Very Inspirational To Me In My Spiritual Journey

Tonight and every night for the rest of your life, I want you to take the last 5 minutes before you go off to sleep and realize that you are about to program your subconscious mind. Your subconscious mind is most at home when you are unconscious when you are asleep. If you spend the last five min of your day which so many people do. Reviewing all the things that you don't like, and all the things that didn't work out, and how terrible you feel, and who abused you and who was mean to you, and who said this and they did this, and you're constantly doing this kind of thing with your mind, then you are programming your subconscious mind that when you awaken because you're now about to marinate for the next eight hours in your subconscious mind.

And then when you awaken, you will rejoin the universal subconscious mind, the mind of God from which we all originate, we're all just individualized, personal expressions of that one thing that we call the Tao or God or Divine Mind or soul or spirit, but the Tao that can be named is not the Tao.

(The Tao or Dao is the natural way of the universe, primarily as conceived by Asian Philosophy and religion. This seeing of life cannot be grasped as a concept.

Rather, it is seen through the actual living experience of one's everyday being. The concept is represented by the Chinese character 道, which has meanings including 'way', 'path', 'road', and sometimes 'doctrine' or 'principle'.

In the Tao Te Ching, Laozi explains that the Tao is not a name for a thing, but the underlying natural order of the universe whose ultimate essence is difficult to circumscribe because it is non-conceptual yet evident in one's being of aliveness. The Tao is "eternally nameless" and should be distinguished from the countless named things that are considered to be its manifestations, the reality of life before its descriptions.)

So you want to be real careful about how you program your subconscious mind.

This is from the Book of Job.

"In a Dream. In a vision of the night when deep sleep falls upon men while slumbering on their beds, then he opens the ears of men and seals their instruction Job 33, 15 and 16.

When you are slumbering on your bed. He opens your ears and seals your instruction.

What you place into your subconscious mind as you are about to go into this deep slumber is all dependent upon what you do the last three or four or five minutes before you go off to sleep. You want to place into your imagination whatever you have placed into the, I AM THAT that I spoke about earlier, I am well, I am content, I am peaceful, I am happy, I am prosperous, I am abundant.

I am God, I am God, I am God because at the basic core, each and every one of us is just that. If you would listen to this meditation. It's from the book "Three Magic Words".

Here's what I'd like you to say to yourself at night. I know that I am pure spirit, that I always have been and that I always will be, there is inside me a place of confidence and quietness and security, where all things are known and understood. This is the universal mind, God of which I am a part and which responds to me as I ask of it.

This universal mind knows the answer to all of my problems and even now the answers are speeding their way to me. I needn't struggle for them; I needn't worry or strive for them. When the time comes, the answers will be there. I give my problems to the great mind of God, I let go of them. Confident that the correct answers will be returned to me when they are needed. Through the great Law of Attraction, everything in life that I need for my work and fulfilment will come to me.

It is not necessary that I strain about this, only believe for in the strength of my belief, my faith will make it so I see the hand of divine intelligence all about me and the flower the tree that broke the meadow. I know that the intelligence that created all these things is in me and around me and that I can call upon it for my slightest need. I know that my body is a manifestation of pure spirit, and the spirit is perfect, therefore my body is perfect also.

I enjoy life, for each day brings a constant demonstration of the power and wonder of the universe and myself I am confident, I am serene, I am sure. No matter what obstacle or undesirable circumstance crosses my path, I refuse to accept it, for it is nothing but illusion. There can be no obstacle or undesirable circumstance to the mind of God, which is in me, around me, and serves me now.

This is a great lesson. Know this within you. When Herman Melville was writing Moby Dick, he wasn't writing about a man looking for a whale. He was writing about a man trying to find his higher self. He said these words.

"For as this appalling ocean. Surrounds the verdant land. Soul, in the soul of man, lies one insular Tahiti, full of peace and joy. But encompassed by all of the horrors of the half-lived life. In every moment of your life, as you leave here today, you have this choice. You can either be a host to God or a hostage to your ego.

It's your call. Thank you. God bless you. Namaste.

Dr Wayne Dyer

(Wayne Walter Dyer (May 10, 1940 – August 29, 2015) was an American self-help author and motivational speaker. Dyer completed an E.D. in guidance and counselling at Wayne State University in 1970. Early in his career, he worked as a high school guidance counsellor and went on to run a successful private therapy practice. He became a popular professor at St John's University, where he was approached by a literary agent to put his ideas into book form. The result was his first book, *Your Erroneous Zones* (1976), one of the best-selling books of all time, with an estimated 100 million copies sold. This launched Dyer's career as a motivational speaker and self-help author, during which he published 20 more best-selling books and produced a number of popular specials for PBS. Influenced by thinkers such

THE POWER OF WORDS, THE INNER VOICE, AND EMOTIONAL RESPONSES

as Abraham Mas, low and Albert Ellis, Dyer's early work focused on psychological themes such as motivation, self-actualization and assertiveness. By the 1990s, the focus of his work had shifted to spirituality. Inspired by Swami Muktananda and New Thought. Dr Dyer promoted themes such as the "power of intention," collaborated with alternative medicine advocate Deepak Chopra on a number of projects, and was a frequent guest on the Oprah Winfrey Show.)

CHAPTER 7
BREAKING THE CYCLE – OVERCOMING NEGATIVE THOUGHT PATTERNS AND DEPRESSIVE OR SUICIDAL THOUGHTS

BREAKING THE CYCLE-OVERCOMING NEGATIVE THOUGHT PATTERNS AND DEPRESSIVE OR SUICIDAL THOUGHTS

Negative thought patterns, or cognitive can manifest as incorrect assumptions, unrealistic self-criticisms, and even self-hate. The effects of this thinking can be all too real for someone struggling with their mental health.

Breaking the cycle of negative thought patterns requires learning how to cope effectively with the feelings and triggers that lead to negative thinking. Someone experiencing mental health struggles can be led into a depressive spiral of negative thoughts by any number of possible triggers—from unhelpful advice to minor or major relationship issues—and those negative thoughts can take on a variety of different forms.

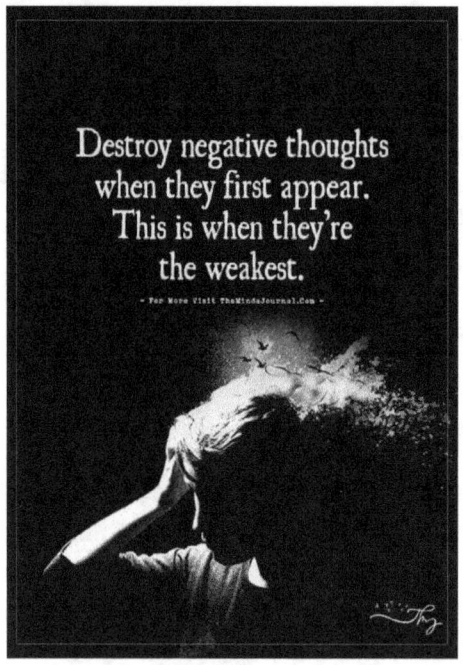

WHAT CAUSES NEGATIVE THOUGHT PATTERNS?

There are many theories as to why human beings sometimes seem so hyper-focused on the negative aspects of our existence. Our culture and media often glorify struggle and conflict. Our evolutionary makeup is based on a need to fight, flight and survive. Even modern human history is in many ways a tale of violence and terror. It is perhaps no wonder we can be so fixated on the negative things around us.

As I write this in August 2024 my country, the United Kingdom, has seen some of the worst rioting in decades, mostly racially motivated and driven by hate and religion.

We are in the second year of the war in Ukraine with Russia and it is nearly a year since Hamas invaded Israel and killed over one thousand Jews. I wonder that if You watch the news you would feel that the world is on a precipice to disaster!!

So what is the main cause of negative thinking? There is no single main cause that we can point to, as negative thinking arises from a complex web of dynamic factors. The primary driver of a negative thought pattern will vary greatly depending on the person engaged in the negative thinking, their particular history, their triggers, and their current mental health situation.

Whatever the true root of our negative thought patterns, we can all take steps to empower ourselves to overcome them and break free of their influence.

Cognitive Distortion: When Negative Thinking forms a Larger Pattern

When harmful patterns of thought occur repeatedly, this meets the definition of a cognitive distortion. The term "distortion" is used because these negative thoughts lead to untrue and unrealistic conclusions or even distortions of reality itself.

In the simplest terms, cognitive distortions are errors in thinking. More specifically, the term refers to insecure, self-destructive, or nihilistic thinking that leads people to hold harmful false beliefs about themselves and their place in the world. This, in turn, can cause or exacerbate mental health issues such as depression and anxiety.

Learning to identify cognitive distortions can help someone break free of them. By recognizing and coping with the issue when the negative thought pattern is first beginning, you have a better chance of disrupting this pattern before it spirals into a larger mental health crisis.

BREAKING THE CYCLE-OVERCOMING NEGATIVE THOUGHT PATTERNS AND DEPRESSIVE OR SUICIDAL THOUGHTS

Common cognitive distortions include thinking yourself unworthy of love or success, believing everyone hates you, blaming yourself for your parents' divorce, and other self-destructive beliefs. Cognitive distortions are not always self-deprecating, however. They can also be projected onto other people and the world around you, such as believing everyone is lying, blaming a person or institution for your personal problems, or obsessing over a partner's feelings towards you. The link between negative thought patterns and depression is not surprising to anyone who has struggled with depression. The relationship between the two is cyclical, almost paradoxical in a chicken-and-egg way. Is being negative a symptom of depression? Yes, but the opposite is also true – depression leads to negative thinking.

Someone suffering from clinical depression, for example, may struggle to find the energy to get out of bed in the morning, even on a good day. Add a negative thought pattern that leads to a sense of hopelessness (e.g., "What's the point of getting out of bed at all when nobody cares about me?"), and you have another significant obstacle impairing the depressed person's ability to function, much less heal.

What Are Examples of Negative Patterns?

Mental health experts have identified many specific types of negative thinking patterns, including:

- Polarization or Dichotomous Thinking:

When complex issues are oversimplified so that they become black or white, yes or no, good versus bad (or me versus them) matters, that's dichotomous thinking. This all-or-nothing mindset makes it hard to approach issues with any sort of nuance or room for compromise. The idea that "there is no second place" (i.e., you must be the absolute best to be considered a success) is a common example of harmful dichotomous thinking.

- Emotional Reasoning:

When a person insists that something is factually true even though their only evidence is their own feelings, they are engaging in emotional reasoning. Someone in the throes of emotional reasoning is difficult to engage with productively because they centre their reasoning around negative emotions rather than any sort of logic. The emotional reasoner starts with the premise that their negative feelings must be true and justified simply because they exist and then builds a narrative to support that. "I'm anxious about going to school, therefore going to school must be dangerous," would be an example of emotional reasoning.

- Overgeneralization:

Overgeneralization means fixating on one negative detail or experience and assigning it an overblown significance in your life. For example, a waiter breaks a glass clearing a table which leads them to exclaim, "I'm the most useless waiter to ever live!" This despairing notion is not proportionate to the event that triggered it. Only by overgeneralizing their entire career in the context of this mundane mistake could someone come to such a conclusion.

- Labelling:

Putting negative labels on yourself and the people and things around you is another very common type of harmful thought pattern that many people engage in every day without really thinking about it. If someone consistently sees themselves as "a loser" or "stupid" or "a bad father," they can eventually grow into that mold because their negative perception leaves them no room to live outside those labels or grow beyond them.

- Jumping to Conclusions:

Most of us have been guilty of a mistaken assumption at some point. However, when someone experiencing mental health struggles jumps to a negative conclusion about something—usually themselves—it can become extremely difficult to correct or change that belief.

- Mental Filtering:

When someone chooses (consciously or otherwise) to remember only the bad parts of a situation, they're engaged in mental filtering. A depressed athlete who forgets their many excellent plays and instead rants about one blown assignment and how it cost their team the game would be an example of mental filtering.

- Fortune-Telling:

Another type of negative thought pattern involves repeatedly predicting that situations will turn out poorly.

Projecting pessimism onto the future can create a self-fulfilling prophecy where your negative vision of the future is so strong it impacts your ability to behave in a way that would lead to positive outcomes. For example, a student with an upcoming test believes they're going to fail, so they don't bother to study, which does indeed lead to a failed test.

- 8 Mind-Reading:

Fortune-telling and mind-reading may sound like amazing psychic abilities, but when we're talking about cognitive distortion, neither of them is particularly helpful. Mind reading in this context means assuming you know exactly what someone else thinks and feels, especially what they think and feel about you. Assuming someone hates you because they gave a short, hurried response to a question (when perhaps they were just flustered by something unrelated) would be an example of negative mind-reading behaviour.

- Magnification or Catastrophizing:

Most of us have been guilty of this in a heated moment. Magnification, sometimes called catastrophizing, simply means blowing an issue out of proportion. Allowing a bad taxi ride to ruin an entire vacation is an example of catastrophizing.

- Inability to Be Wrong:

Everyone likes to feel correct, but this desire becomes a cognitive distortion when the need to be right outweighs evidence, logic, and material reality. Growth—including the growth needed for mental health recovery—requires allowing yourself the room to be forgiven and to grow. If you can never be incorrect in the first place, there's no space for that growth to occur.

- Control Fallacies:

A control fallacy can manifest in two possible forms. One is that you despair because you have no control over anything in your life and are therefore powerless to change it. The other is that you despair because you have absolute control over everything in your life and are therefore entirely to blame for any negative or difficult circumstances.

- Fairness Fallacies:

The age-old adage "the world's not fair" is usually spoken in response to someone struggling with a fairness fallacy. Analyzing situations in terms of how just or unjust they are might be a worthwhile socio-political exercise, but it's often not helpful in the context of personal mental health.

- Change Fallacies:

Believing or assuming that someone or something will eventually change to suit your needs is a fallacy of change. This is essentially a matter of projecting your own needs and desires onto the world around you.

- Minimizing or Discounting:

Not all negative thought patterns are actually centred on negative thoughts. Another form of cognitive distortion occurs when someone fails to appreciate positive things in their life and instead ignores or marginalizes them. This refusal to acknowledge the good allows negative feelings to flourish unchecked. Writing off all of your accomplishments as "luck" is an example of minimizing.

- Personalization and Self-Blame:

When you take issues or details that have nothing to do with you and make them all about yourself, your feelings, or your role in matters, you are experiencing the cognitive distortion called personalization. A ubiquitous example of personalization is a child blaming themselves for their parents getting divorced.

- Imperatives:

Framing things in terms like "should" or "must" can be a big part of negative thinking. For example, someone who gets nervous talking on the telephone might berate themselves because they believe they "should" be able to make a simple phone call without feeling anxious. This minimizes their ability to accept that it's okay to feel anxious, and in turn, prevents them from doing the work of actually coping with anxiety. Instead, they remain uselessly distraught that the anxiety exists at all.

Not every pattern of negative thought will fit neatly into one of the above definitions, and oftentimes two or more forms of cognitive distortion will manifest together. In other cases, one type of negative thinking will lead directly to another, creating larger and more complex patterns that can require a lot of hard work and support to break.

Habits that Lead to Cognitive Distortion

[Working on your mental health](#) involves identifying patterns within patterns. There are some attitudes and mental habits you may be bringing into your day-to-day life that lead to cycles of negative thought. You can help yourself by learning to recognize them as they occur and stop them before they lead to a negative place.

1. Overthinking:

It's good to be thorough when making important choices, but if you can't decide where to go for lunch because you're wracked by insecurity and doubt, you're engaging in a harmful thought pattern. Overthinking involves looking at your role in every decision from every possible angle and trying to model every potential outcome in your mind. This can be exhausting at best and devastating if your carefully considered predictions turn out completely wrong. Avoid overthinking by imposing limits on it. Give yourself deadlines for making choices and stick to them. You can also try yoga, working out, or [breathing exercises](#) for a healthy way to drive some of that excess thought from your head.

2. Rumination:

BREAKING THE CYCLE-OVERCOMING NEGATIVE THOUGHT PATTERNS AND DEPRESSIVE OR SUICIDAL THOUGHTS

Self-reflection and self-awareness can be beautiful things, but if your thought process is distorted by negativity and depression, they can be devastating. Do you find yourself dwelling on flaws and mistakes instead of ways to improve things? Negative rumination is itself a cyclical pattern that projects your flaws onto your vision of the future, making you believe that your life will only get worse. Break the cycle by doing something else when you first notice yourself fixating on negative thoughts. Don't allow yourself to be alone with your thoughts. Read a book, watch a movie, work on a hobby, or visit with a friend (but don't simply use them as a convenient outlet for the negative thoughts in your own head). Avoid food and alcohol as diversions. Overeating and intoxication can worsen the situation.

3. Cynical Hostility:

Cynical hostility is a type of thought pattern that involves directing anger, mistrust, judgment, or disdain at other people. These feelings may be borne of insecurity, projection, or past baggage. This type of thinking makes it hard to maintain a support system because you see people as inherently dangerous, evil, or untrustworthy. Studies have linked this sort of hostile demeanour to heart disease and increased blood pressure. Combat cynical hostility with empathy. Instead of defaulting to distrust, try to see a situation from every possible perspective. Find ways to re-frame situations as cooperative rather than competitive.

Breaking Negative Thinking Patterns

Healthy Coping Mechanisms:

- **Schedule your negative thinking.** Deliberately setting aside time in your day to have negative thoughts may seem counterproductive, but doing it in a structured, routine way allows you to compartmentalize and most past your negative feelings rather than wallow in them. Keep a negative thought journal and give yourself a 10- or 15-minute block each day to simply feel those feelings.

- **Replace the bad thoughts.** Easier said than done, replacing negative thoughts is a habit that requires practice and repetition for success. You must learn to identify when negative thought patterns begin, disrupt them, and replace them with a pleasant or productive thought that you've chosen ahead of time and have in mind.

- **Love yourself.** Some studies show that up to 90% of "self-talk" is negative talk. Feel your negative and insecure feelings, but don't dwell on them. Instead of criticizing yourself, imagine yourself as your own best friend, either a real one or an ideal best friend you've built in your mind. Instead of pitiful self-talk, envision how this friend would speak to you about the issues you're having and find ways to uplift and encourage you.

- **Keep a journal.** Keep a notebook or document for your negative thoughts. Write down the thought, then write down why you believe you're having that thought and any word associations you might have along with it. Getting things down on the page helps you organize and analyses your thoughts and feelings more productively than simply running them through your mind in circles.

- **Find the beauty in the world.** Sometimes breaking negative thought patterns can be as simple as reminding yourself of the good things in the world. Make time for the things you enjoy and the people you love.

- **Be honest with yourself.** Often negative thoughts and defense mechanisms are wrapped up in complex systems. For example, if you dwell on a parenting mistake to justify an extreme and despairing belief that you're the worst parent ever, you can avoid looking at the more complex and serious issue of how you could improve your parenting style. Be willing to ask yourself difficult questions and allow yourself patience and understanding when the answers are complicated or uncomfortable.

- **Take a break from the news and social media.** The outside world can be overwhelming, especially when you're invested in working on yourself. It's okay to shut it off and have some "me time." An encyclopedic knowledge of current events isn't necessary, and even in this plugged-in world, you don't owe anybody 24/7 availability at the expense of your own mental health.

- **Exercise and meditation.** Learning skills to keep your brain quiet and your body active can play a crucial role in breaking negative thought patterns. Yoga and breathing exercises are particularly useful.

In summary, a depressed mood can color the way we remember our personal past and lead to biased memory of negative events. Memories of negative past events may become key reference points through which people with depression view themselves. When people with depression remember negative past events, they may attach negative meaning to them and become highly self-critical. Different therapies can help reverse the downward spiral of depressed mood, negative memories, and self-criticism.

Most people experience passing periods of sadness or negative feelings in their everyday lives. Normally, these feelings are relatively short-lived and do not have a long-lasting impact on how people view themselves and the world. However, during depression, negative thoughts and feelings of sadness may become all-encompassing and end up colouring every aspect of people's lives: past as well as present. This is reflected in the tendency of depressed individuals to more easily remember negative than positive past events, while healthy individuals typically remember more positive than negative events from their past. Unpleasant feelings related to negative events may also fade slower than normal, and thinking about negative events causes heightened levels of distress and negative emotions during depression. This heightened salience of negative past events and difficulties dealing with these memories may profoundly impact the everyday mood of individuals suffering from depression and interfere with recovery from depression.

But why do negative memories become more salient during depression? How do these memories maintain depression? And is there anything that can be done to make negative memories less salient and distressing, and heighten memory for positive past events?

We remember events that are aligned with our present mood. Our autobiographical memory can be understood as an enormous network of representations of events from our own lives. In this network, representations of events that share characteristics are linked together by associative pathways. This can be of huge help in everyday life. For example, in everyday life, we encounter multiple situations that are slightly different from any situation we have encountered in our past. If we had to learn from scratch how to deal with every new situation, this would require a great deal of time and cognitive resources. Luckily, because our memory links together conceptually related events, we can relatively easily recall and utilize the knowledge acquired from related past situations to help us deal with new situations, even if they are not exactly the same.

However, this heightened accessibility of related events also means that, if we are in a specific mood or state, we will be more likely to remember past events that are consistent with that mood than memories that are not aligned with our current mood. During depression, when the prevailing feeling is one of profound sadness, this prompting of mood-aligned material might lead to excessive activation of memories of negative past events. This excessive activation of negative memories may in turn lead to a further mood deterioration and ultimately result in a downward spiral where negative memories and moods reinforce each other and maintain a depressed mood.

Negative memories become more ingrained in our identity. Memories of past events play an important role in defining our identity and life stories. Healthy adults generally view positive past events as more central to their identity and life stories than negative past events. This greater integration of positive, relative to negative, life events in one's identity has a self-enhancing effect and is associated with greater life satisfaction. When people suffer from depression, however, they often view negative past events as more central to their life stories. This means that, during depression, negative life events may become key reference points through which people view themselves and their present life situation, and may create a more negative outlook on the future. This is likely to maintain a depressed mood by reinforcing a negative view of the world and oneself.

We become harsh evaluators of ourselves and our past. One of the key characteristics of depressive thinking is rumination or a repetitive and evaluative focus on one's thoughts and emotions. These evaluations are often highly negative and self-critical and may become so habitual during depression that they seem almost impossible to escape. Often, these evaluations may seem logical to people suffering from depression. Indeed, many people with depression report using rumination as an attempt to cope with or understand their depression and their past. However, in reality, the negative and self-critical nature of these evaluations means that they often lead to a worsening mood and a heightened sense of hopelessness. This is also true for the evaluations that people with depression make about their memories of negative past events.

When people with high levels of depression have intrusive memories of unpleasant past events, they are more likely to attach negative meaning to these memories, such as thinking that something is wrong with themselves or that they are inadequate, compared to people with low levels of depression. They also think more about what they could have done differently and worry that the event could happen again. These negative, self-focused evaluations of past events may lead to heightened emotional distress when thinking about an unpleasant past event, and as such have a considerable impact on the everyday mood and well-being of individuals with depression.

While it is clear that depression negatively colours the way we view our past and that this can lead to a negative spiral where a depressed mood is maintained, this does not mean that there is no way of reversing the spiral. Researchers and psychologists have developed several techniques and therapies that may reduce intrusive negative memories or help people with depression deal with or relate to their memories in more adaptive ways. One technique that may help people deal with upsetting memories is 'Imagery Rescripting.' When used in therapeutic settings to deal with upsetting memories, this technique involves reliving the upsetting memories in our minds and then rewriting them in ways that make them less upsetting. For example, we may imagine comforting or standing up for our past selves against a bully. This may help us view our past selves with greater compassion and dignity, rather than viewing ourselves as worthless or powerless.

Working with upsetting representations of past events in this way may also reduce their intrusiveness because they are replaced by less disturbing representations through the process of imagery rescripting.

Other therapies that may help people deal with negative memories are therapies that encourage people to relate to their mental content in new and more adaptive ways, such as mindfulness-based cognitive therapy (MBCT). One of the key skills encouraged by these therapies is the ability to mentally step back and perceive our mental content in an open, accepting, and non-judgmental manner. This may help us become more accepting of the experience of having upsetting memories and reduce automatic and negative evaluations when we think about our past. By changing how we evaluate and relate to our negative memories, the negative mood impact of these memories may be dampened.

In addition to these techniques that may reduce intrusions and negative evaluations of upsetting memories, researchers have also identified a technique that may help people with depression access positive memories more easily. This technique includes utilizing the 'method-of-loci' technique. This involves individuals imagining a familiar route or location consisting of rich and vivid imagery to which they can attach memories of positive events, as well as rich and vivid elaborations of the positive events. The rich imagery and elaboration encouraged by this technique may both improve the ability to recall positive memories in people with depression and have beneficial effects on mood.

Although depression can lead people down a spiral of heightened access to negative memories, self-critical evaluations, and mood deterioration, there are ways of reversing this spiral. Different therapies and techniques may help people with depression relate to their upsetting memories in less judgmental

BREAKING THE CYCLE-OVERCOMING NEGATIVE THOUGHT PATTERNS AND DEPRESSIVE OR SUICIDAL THOUGHTS

and more self-affirming ways, through rescripting and encouraging a more accepting stance towards the memories and oneself. Furthermore, available techniques that can make it easier to access rich and vivid representations of positive past events may increase positive emotions in individuals with depression. These changes can have a powerful impact on the everyday mood and perceptions of people with depression and help lift them out of a negative depressive spiral.

Remember, You are in control and You can switch your mood immediately, You do not have to wait. The universe loves speed and wants you to be happy, remember that. We are beings made up of emotions and feelings, control these to your advantage and miracles happen I can assure You, I know because I have been at both ends of the spectrum. We have a choice. Live a purposeful, loving enjoyable and productive life or give up and join the scrap heap of humanity, it's your choice.

Chapter 8
The Power Of Self-Belief & Positive Actions

Every single dream, vision or idea in your life starts with an understanding that what you are going to do to make it obtainable, that you can make it real, that is the beginning of everything. Self-belief is the gatekeeper that stands between your current situation and your ideal future. If you think of reality as the city walls you're living in, it's not silly to think that they're going to be people that only know that existence within the walls. That's what they see. That's why most self-limiting beliefs shackle you.

It is only self-belief, a confidence in something greater outside those walls, that opens the gate, that expands your reality. You don't believe anything good exists on the other side, why? If you don't believe you're capable of getting there, why start? And this formula is very straightforward. Let's not overthink it. We must only move towards outcomes that we believe to be possible, and that's more important than ability, skill set, strength, you name it. Believing in yourself trumps all and that's because the person with an inferior skill set, maybe an average natural talent, but they believe in something and they move towards it, they give everything for this idea, they know it to be true.

The very talented persons that's unsure, they procrastinate, they are half in and half out and do not take the massive action required for getting the success and results they desire. And if you don't believe in yourself, you're building a city on sand, with no stable foundation. Great things and results are great for a reason. They are in rare supply. They are limited, which means not everyone can have them which means those who do have them have to fight for them, have to deal with being uncomfortable, have to give more, sacrifice more, pay a steeper price than the masses, there's something different.

And if you don't look in the mirror, stare yourself in the face, and know you are one of those select few what is going to happen when life kicks back at you, it's your fault, you resort back to what you know. You'll flee the battle for safety, security and comfort. When you know your movie ends at the top of the mountain, when you know at the end of the day you're going to cross a finish line or hold a trophy, your brain internalizes the conflict very differently than just accepting failure. Very differently for someone with self-believe obstacles who don't think they can make it. You already know you have to keep going, I mean, come on, you haven't arrived yet. Don't get stuck, don't get caught in the trap. In this situation, obstacles simply prompt you to ask how, how can I get through this and that's the small discrepancy that changes everything. Because at some point you'll look to your right, and you'll look to your left, and you'll find very few people get to the how question. They all stopped it. If I wonder if I can do this, I wonder if I'm capable, well they'll never know. They'll never see that sunset beyond those metaphorical city walls because they never truly believed in themselves they never opened that gate.

Most of the world quits when things get challenging. If you don't, if you have the courage to believe in trust and in yourself, You WILL SUCCEED. Why? Because you won't stop until you find a way. That's the power of self-belief. It's not quantum physics, it's not complex. You know at one point, I didn't think I could make a living outside of a nine-to-five job or previously as a serving police officer following all the rules and taking orders from my superiors. It was not for me and thank goodness I was injured on duty and retired. How you go from police officer, to author, then fund manager is the stuff of dreams but I did it because of self-belief, a vision and a written plan. Now my written plan is based on my trading and investing career, however as you will see from the excerpt below it starts with some life basics that have served me extremely well. I very highly recommend you WRITE DOWN your short-term, medium-term term and long-term objectives and dreams and aspirations because this focuses on the mind, the energy and creates the self-belief. Here is the excerpt from my plan.

My Purpose

My purpose is to empower my fellow traders and investors with the knowledge, belief and confidence instilled in me by the master, Tom Williams. I want all who connect with me to be consistently profitable in the markets, be happy and help others know the truth about the markets, the herd and the smart money. I want to share my knowledge and experiences of using the Law of Attraction and Self-Belief which has been so important in my life.

YOU GET PAID TO WAIT / BE PATIENT

BELIEVE AND YOU WILL RECEIVE

WE DON'T RECEIVE WISDOM, WE MUST DISCOVER IT FOR OURSELVES AFTER A JOURNEY THAT NO ONE ELSE CAN TAKE FOR US OR SPARE US.

I AM ABLE TO SUCCEED IN ANYTHING I DECIDE TO DO; THIS IS THE TRUTH BUT I MUST BELIEVE IT.

Mission Statement

- I am very grateful for everything I have today and gratefully expect more to come.
- I will share the information imparted to me by the late Tom Williams with my fellow brothers and sisters who seek me or who connect with me.
- I will make money in the markets and assist others to do the same.
- I will excel at trading and will become a hedge fund manager in 2 years.

- I will act with integrity, honesty and fairness in all my dealings with others.

- I will achieve my monthly and yearly financial goals and will always control my own destiny.

- I will travel the world and teach what I know to others so they too may become financially independent.

- I will connect with other like-minded people who have the same desires and aspirations that I have.

My Mission

To live a purposeful, meaningful and enjoyable life and enjoy all I have and graciously seek more of what I want. To love my friends and family and be a good husband, father, brother, son, boss, friend and teacher. To understand that the universe is abundant and to know that every single person on this earth is important and should be treated as such. To understand and master the universal laws and always connect with the higher power and know that I can empower myself and others to have a great life.

Always remember:

BULLS MAKE MONEY!

BEARS MAKE MONEY!

PIGS GET SLAUGHTERED!!!

MONEY NEVER SLEEPS!

Remember Ali Baba and the forty thieves – don't be greedy!!

SWOT Analysis

Strengths

- I have knowledge, the skill and the patience to succeed in the markets.

- I am able to read the charts and follow the smart money.

- If I was to lose my account it would not affect my lifestyle or cause financial hardship.

- I have the support of my wife in my trading.

- I have created multiple income streams through businesses and investments

- I BELIEVE in myself and am grateful for the abilities I have.

Weaknesses

- I can still be impatient and sometimes I lose focus.

- I sometimes try to multitask which I am not good at.

- I can overtrade and I need to recognize this when it is happening.

Opportunities

- I am in a financially stable position and each year have gone from strength to strength.

- Through the knowledge imparted to me by Tom Williams, I have created many opportunities and have connected with some wonderful people.

- I know the universe is abundant and that I can have everything I desire if I believe and take MASSIVE ACTION on my thoughts of prosperity and happiness.

Threats

I foresee no threats to my future and live each day in eager anticipation of more great things to come.

I was very fortunate in the late nineties to meet my mentor and guide, Tom George Williams by chance (although I now know it was my destiny). Tom was a former syndicate trader in Beverley Hills, California, and he retired at forty as a very wealthy man. He returned to the UK and developed the software program, TradeGuider VSA, the company I own and run today. It is now thirty-six years old, no mean feat in these turbulent times. Tom was

THE POWER OF SELF-BELIEF & POSITIVE ACTIONS

not religious but he was very spiritual and we spent hundreds of hours together at his home in Worthing in Southern England.

We would spend hours together, often in his garden in the summer as I cooked the Barbeque for his partner, Dallas Badham and Tom. I remember once we discussed the intelligence of Mother Nature. He pointed at the very large oak tree in his garden and he said "Gav, that tree has been here for hundreds of years, and it knows when to drop its leaves and acorns in the Autumn and grow them all back in the spring. The intelligence in that tree and in all of nature is in us but we do not appreciate that as human beings, we feel separate but we are not, we are all one with the intelligence that created this planet billions of years ago. Connect with the higher power, god or supreme being whatever you wish to call this force and ask for what you need, for it will be given to you with the right beliefs. Always be grateful Gav, because gratitude and love drive humanity drive us all. Now let's go and have a laugh at the news, put on BBC News and watch the grim-faced reporter looking into the camera saying the news is bad, and it's getting worse."

Tom taught me very early on there is no news in good news. We seem to be constantly bombarded by news of war, criminal activity, earthquakes, tsunamis, riots, mass shootings, etc. One day, Tom and I were listening to BBC Radio Five Live and the presenter said for the next three hours we are only going to report good news so please call in with any good news for our listeners. Her voice really perked up when the first caller said my daughter gave birth to healthy twin boys this morning. The next caller said he had just received the all-clear from a cancer diagnosis. This went on and was the most uplifting program I had ever listened to. After three hours the presenter announced it was back to normal and her voice dropped and went back to almost a depressed tone as she started to read all the bad news again.

Mark Twain said "If you don't read the newspaper you are uninformed, if you do read the newspaper you are misinformed. The world is full of beauty and miracles, look and you will find it.

Next day, the headline in the Daily Mail, a popular newspaper in the United Kingdom had the headline "THE NEWS IS BAD AND ITS GETTING WORSE"!!

Thank You Tom for everything you did for me and I dedicate this book to you and your memory, you were truly unique, one of a kind and my inspiration to succeed in both trading and investing and in life.

Tom George Willaims "The Master"

(4ᵗʰ January 1929 – November 7ᵗʰ 2016)

For the first time in my life, I believed anything was possible. I changed my actions to support my beliefs, and here we are. At one point, I didn't think certain financial goals were reality, I didn't know about a free, flexible lifestyle. Wasn't aware of the type of relationships that would change my life. Why? Because they existed outside those city walls, I didn't believe they were real, I didn't believe in myself. To create them, to make them in my own life, but with the change in belief comes a change in reality. You will always follow through on who you believe you are.

So let's go back to that nerve visualization at some point today, look at your reflection and think about nothing. What I'm about to tell you, everything you need, you have, I promise you, you are equipped to change your life, the lives of everyone around you in the world in which you exist So take that back. Do it and never ask it again from now on, the question is how your fate is not A-A coin flip it's a puzzle, it's about arranging the pieces and those two eyes looking back at you are more than capable of figuring that out. Ask simply, do you want it and if yes, open that front door, take that first step and inject yourself into a journey that will be unlike anything you have ever experienced before. You have the answers, the aptitude, and now the self-belief, and when you find yourself in the lowest of lows, or the darkest of nights find solace in that fact that you have the power, you are in control, in fact, you have enough electricity within to power a small town. Use the power wisely and be grateful for the gift of life and the knowledge and experiences that come with it. You are a being of light if you choose the path to enlightenment. Remember this, your mind is like a parachute, it's best used when you open it.

Some wise words from the great Albert Einstein whom I have studied closely to try to work out what makes a genius and discovered I am not in that category, yet!!

Here are five things you should never share with anyone. Albert Einstein once said, everyone has problems, but if yours becomes too alarming, others will abandon their own issues to focus on yours. Some things are meant to be shared, but others should remain private, regardless of how close you are to someone. Einstein said there are five key things because if you can keep these private, other aspects of your life will fall into place. Let's explore the five things you should never share, according to Albert Einstein.

Number one - don't share the secret of your success. This doesn't mean you can't inspire or motivate others with your achievements, however, it's not advisable to divulge the secrets behind your success to everyone in our world. It's hard to know people's true intentions, while there are good people out there, it's to your advantage to go about your business without revealing the specifics of what makes you successful. If you disclose your success secrets, others might try to replicate your methods, and if they fail, they might blame you for misleading them. So never reveal the secret of your success.

Number two - don't share your problems with just anyone. Sharing our problems can make us feel lighter, but it doesn't necessarily solve them. In fact, telling others about your issues can sometimes make them worse. A large percentage of people are happy to hear about your troubles, while only a small percentage genuinely care. Think twice before discussing your problems with others. When you share your problems, you open yourself up to being a subject of gossip. Many people don't care about your issues, and some might even be pleased that you have them. Best course of action is to find ways to solve your problems on your own, without exposing them to others, unless you're seeking professional advice from a doctor or therapist.

Number three, don't share your dreams with anyone. If you have set goals and dreams, it's best to keep them to yourself. Sharing your dreams can alter your perspective and purpose, causing you to get caught up in others' opinions. Remember, you won't receive the same advice or viewpoint from everyone. As each person has a different perspective, your dreams may seem insignificant or even laughable to others. They might see darkness where you see light. Opinions vary and not everyone needs to agree with you. Keep your dreams private and work on them consistently until they become a reality.

Number four - don't share how much you earn. Your income is something that should remain private. If you go around sharing details about your earnings and finances, you may attract unnecessary envy. Your income and financial matters should be known only to you. If you need financial advice, seek it from the appropriate authorities, not your friends or acquaintances.

Number five - don't share your family problems with anyone. Every family has issues, some big, and some small, however, sharing these problems with others won't solve them, it will only exacerbate them. Family problems should remain within the family; no third party should be involved. Every family has its unique challenges, but if yours becomes too alarming others will focus on your issues instead of their own. While many things should be kept private, these five are particularly important. If you can keep these aspects of your life private, other things will naturally fall into place.

Wise Words from Einstein

- Weak people want revenge. Strong people forgive. Intelligent people ignore.

- The difference between stupidity and genius is that genius has its limits.

- Don't listen to the person who has the answers. Listen to the person who has the questions.

- If you want to live a happy life, tie it to a goal, not to people? Or, things? Success comes from curiosity, concentration, perseverance and self-criticism.

- The only thing more dangerous than ignorance is arrogance. A person who has never made a mistake, has never tried anything new. Experience is knowledge. Everything else is information. Learn from yesterday, live for today, hope for tomorrow? The important thing is not to stop questioning.

- The more I study science, the more I believe in God. Everything that exists in your life does so because of two things, something you did or something you didn't do.

- Don't wait for miracles. Your whole life is a miracle.

- If you can't explain it simply, you don't understand it well enough.

- We cannot solve our problems with the same thinking we used when we created them.

- It is the supreme art of the teacher to awaken joy and creative expression and knowledge.

- When you trip over love, it is easy to get up. When you fall in love, it is impossible to stand again.

- Three great forces rule the world, stupidity, fear and greed. The world we have created is a product of our thinking. It cannot be changed without changing our, thinking.

- Life is like riding a bicycle. To keep your balance, you must Keep moving.

- Failure is success in progress. You can't use an old map to explore a new world. Be a voice, not an echo. Great spirits have always encountered opposition from mediocre minds.

- Genius is 1 % talent and 99 % hard work. Intelligence is not the ability to store information, but to know where to find it.

- Only two things are infinite, the universe and human stupidity, and I'm not sure about the universe.

- We cannot get to where we dream of being tomorrow unless we change our thinking today.

- If you want different results, do not do the same things over and over again.

- Whoever is careless with the truth and small matters, cannot be trusted in Important, affairs?

- There are three rules of work. Avoid clutter, find simplicity from discord, find harmony in what you do.

- In the middle of difficulty lies opportunity.

- Peace cannot be kept by force. It can only be achieved by understanding.

- Try not to become a person of success, but rather become a person of value.

- You never fail until you stop trying. The measure of intelligence is the ability to change.

- If I had only one hour to save the world, I would spend 55 minutes defining the problem and only 5 minutes finding the solution. Logic will get you from A to B. Imagination will get you everywhere.

- Insanity is doing the same thing over and over again and expecting different results. Genius is making complex ideas simple, not making simple ideas complex.

- Information is not knowledge. The only source of knowledge is experience. You need experience to gain wisdom.

- Thinking is hard work, that's why so few do it. The height of stupidity is most clearly demonstrated by the individual who ridicules something they know nothing about.

- You have to color outside the lines once in a while if you want to make your life a masterpiece.

- If you want your children to be intelligent, read them fairy tales. If you want them to be more intelligent, read them more fairy tales.

- The more I learn, the more I realize I don't know.

- Don't let your brain interfere with your heart.

- The world is a dangerous place to live, not because of the people who are evil, but because of the people who don't do anything about it.

- Coincidence is God's way of remaining anonymous.

- You have to learn the rules of the game, and then you have to play better than anyone else.

- Blind belief in authority is the greatest enemy of truth.

- When the solution is simple, God is answering.

- I am neither especially clever nor especially gifted. I am only passionately curious.

- Never trust the people who tell you other people's secrets.

CHAPTER 9
AS A MAN OR WOMEN THINKETH, SO SHALL THEY REAP

As a man, think of James Allen, is a work of art published in 1903. It will help you develop a growth mindset. I consider it one of the most powerful books on the planet because its message lies at the foundation of 99 % of all self-development books ever published.

Your Mind Is Like a Garden. A man or woman's mind may be like into a garden, which may be intelligently cultivated or allowed to run wild. But whether cultivated or neglected, it must, and will bring forth. If no useful seeds are put into it, then an abundance of useless weed seeds will fall there and will continue to produce their kind. James tells us that our lives will always be found to be related to our inner state, we are where we are in our lives because of our thoughts as we have discussed in earlier chapters.

If you're unhappy and living in a box under the stairs with no money, it's because of your thoughts. As Bill Gates says, if you were born poor, it's not your fault, if you die poor, it is your fault, so start cultivating your mind by planting useful seeds. To me, this means constantly learning, taking action and thinking better thoughts.

The body is a servant of the mind. Think of unlawful thoughts, the body sinks rapidly into disease and decay, and the command of glad and beautiful thoughts, it becomes clothed with youthfulness and beauty. The difference, between a miserable overweight person and a happy, fit person, is their thoughts. It is not pushing myself to exercise every day, but it makes me happy and fills me with energy. I live in the New Forest National Park on the south coast of England and I am truly blessed to live in such a beautiful part of the world. I have two cocker spaniels, and I make sure to walk at least two miles every day with my dogs. It is not unusual to see wild horses, pigs, donkeys and sheep roaming freely around the park, including on the roads which can be a hazard. We also have many deer that love to jump out into the road at dusk!!

The long-term payoff is worth it. I love eating healthy food every day because I value my health and body. Sometimes, on the other hand, I may think I can't be bothered exercising today so I won't. A bit of fast food for dinner won't hurt me. I've tried exercising and eating healthy for one week but it never made a difference. Of course, you can't think you will be healthy and magically lose weight, but in the last four months I have lost twenty pounds and my BMI is a very healthy 22.3

You cannot become happy overnight, but the habits and actions required to do so all start with the right thoughts.

This brings us to our next lesson. Thought crystallizes into habit, and habit solidifies, into circumstance. On a daily basis, I think about growing a huge YouTube channel that teaches both traders and investors of all levels the truth about the financial markets and how they are rigged against the small guy. Now my mission is to grow the Think, Link, Create community and bring like-minded individuals from all walks of life in multiple countries to share knowledge and power through webinars, seminars and newsletters. I am on the case.

The book, "As a Man Thinketh", doesn't tell us how to form habits, but here are some of the tools I use today in my own life. Before I go to sleep, I make a point each night to listen to Dr. Wayne Dyers "Every Night For The Rest Of Your Life" YouTube video. It is five minutes long but has had a major impact on the way I wake up and spend my day. I very rarely have a bad day, and if I do it's because I went to sleep with an attitude!!

When I awaken, I write my thoughts down first thing in the morning. I write daily affirmations in my journal. An affirmation is basically a thought that you affirm to yourself. The book gives us some very insightful knowledge that I can assure you from my own experiences definitely get results. Many New Age teachers drum into us the power of positive thinking and positive actions, but you need to apply the knowledge in this and many other great books on the subject of Law of Attraction and tapping the source of the energy force that we are in twenty-four hours a day, seven days a week, three hundred and sixty-five days each year. When you learn there is a lot more than we know then you become a sponge and absorb all the information that is coming your way. This book may be the start for you or you may have read many books on the subject of Law of Attraction.

One of the earliest works on this subject was written by Wallace Wattles.

Wallace Delois Wattles(1860 – 7 February 1911) was an American New Thought writer. He remains personally somewhat obscure,[1] but his writing has been widely quoted and remains in print in the New Thought and self-help movements.

Wattles' best-known work is a 1910 book called *The Science of Getting Rich* in which he explains how to become wealthy. This is one of the first books I read nearly twenty years ago.

Wattles practised the technique of creative visualization. In his daughter Florence's words, he "formed a mental picture" or visual image, and then "worked toward the realization of this vision".

He wrote almost constantly. It was then that he formed his mental picture. He saw himself as a successful writer, a personality of power, an advancing man, and he began to work toward the realization of this vision. He lived every page... His life was truly a powerful life. I highly recommend you get the book, it is out of copyright and available freely on the internet as a PDF that can be printed.

James Allen discusses much of what Wattles posturized in The Science of Getting Rich.

- The Power of Thought in Shaping Reality
- The Relationship Between Thought and Circumstance

AS A MAN OR WOMEN THINKETH SO SHALL THEY REAP

- <u>Responsibility for One's Own Life and Destiny</u>
- <u>The Importance of Serenity and Inner Peace</u>
- As a Man Thinketh main points to take away.

Thoughts and Character: Allen begins by stating that thoughts are central to the formation of a person's character. Just as a plant springs from a seed, so does a person's character grow from the thoughts they cultivate. He emphasizes that pure thoughts lead to a pure life, while impure thoughts lead to a life of impurity.

Effect of Thought on Circumstances: In this section, Allen argues that thoughts don't just shape character; they also influence a person's circumstances. People who think positively can shape their circumstances for the better. On the contrary, negative thinking leads to negative circumstances.

Effect of Thought on Health and Body: Allen also explores the connection between mind and body. He suggests that thoughts of fear, jealousy, and anger will manifest themselves physically, causing disease and discomfort. Positive thoughts, however, will create a healthy body.

Thought and Purpose: The author emphasizes the importance of having a purpose in life. Having a strong sense of purpose channels thought into action and allows one to achieve success. Aimlessness, on the other hand, leads to failure.

The Thought Factor in Achievement: Allen stresses that success is not a matter of luck or circumstance. Instead, it's about hard work, focus, and persistent thinking in the right direction. Talent alone is not enough; it's one's thoughts and attitude that determine success.

Visions and Ideals: This chapter deals with the importance of having a vision or ideal to work towards. By focusing on a vision, one can transform it into reality. The author likens it to an artist painting a picture – first conceiving the idea in the mind and then expressing it on the canvas.

Serenity: In the final chapter, Allen talks about achieving inner peace or serenity through right thinking. He argues that calmness of mind is one of the beautiful jewels of wisdom, attainable through understanding and control over one's thoughts.

The Power of Thought In Shaping Reality

Allen's central thesis is that a person's thoughts govern their actions, reactions, and overall life trajectory.

He emphasizes that thoughts are not merely reflections but constructive forces that shape our lives.

For example, he writes,

"A man is literally what he thinks, his character being the complete sum of all his thoughts."

In practical terms, a person who thinks positively and constructively about their goals is more likely to take purposeful actions that lead to success. Conversely, negative and disorganized thinking can lead to a lack of direction and fulfilment.

The Relationship Between Thought and Circumstance

Allen explains that our thoughts not only shape our actions but also the circumstances in which we find ourselves.

He argues that the outer conditions of a person's life will always reflect their inner beliefs.

Allen notes that a man's mind may be likened to a garden, which may be intelligently cultivated or allowed to run wild.

By carefully cultivating one's thoughts, a person can create circumstances that are conducive to their well-being and growth.

Conversely, allowing destructive thoughts to proliferate can lead to unfavourable circumstances.

Responsibility for One's Own Life and Destiny

Allen places a great emphasis on personal responsibility, highlighting the idea that each individual is the architect of their own life and destiny.

He strongly argues against the notion of being a victim of circumstances, suggesting that blaming external factors for one's failures is a refusal to accept personal responsibility.

He writes,

"Men do not attract that which they want, but that which they are."

This emphasizes that who we are internally (our thoughts, beliefs, and attitudes) determines our external reality.

Rather than relying on external forces, Allen encourages readers to recognize that they have the power and responsibility to shape their own paths.

An example here might be an individual who transcends a difficult upbringing by adopting a strong, positive mindset, thereby creating a successful and fulfilling life.

This lesson underscores the empowering concept that individuals have control over their own thoughts, and therefore, their destiny, regardless of external circumstances.

The Importance of Serenity and Inner Peace

Allen also explores the value of calmness and inner peace, viewing them not as mere by-products of a successful life but as essential elements in achieving a fulfilling existence.

Subscribe to Books That Slay!

Get updates on the latest posts and more from Books That Slay straight to your inbox.

He posits that inner tranquillity is achieved through the control and mastery of one's thoughts.

Allen states:

"Calmness of mind is one of the beautiful jewels of wisdom. It is the result of long and patient effort in self-control."

Achieving this level of calmness requires ongoing effort and self-awareness, but it leads to a more balanced and contented life.

A practical application of this lesson might be adopting mindfulness practices to foster serenity and enhance decision-making abilities.

The book "Think and Grow Rich" is often considered a [classic](#) in the self-help genre, and its principles have influenced many personal development teachings since its publication. Allen's style is philosophical and reflective, providing readers with a concise guide to controlling their thoughts, cultivating good habits, and living a life filled with peace and purpose.

The underlying message of "As a Man Thinketh" is clear and resonant: a person's thoughts, whether positive or negative, will shape their life, and by controlling those thoughts, one can master their destiny.

After reading" As a Man Thinketh" the next book I studied was "The Book of Five Rings" by Kenjutsu.

The Book of Five Rings is a text on kenjutsu and martial arts in general, written by the Japanese swordsman Miyamoto Musashi around 1645. Many translations have been made, and it has garnered broad attention in East Asia and throughout the world. For instance, some foreign business leaders find its discussion of conflict to be relevant to their work. The modern-day Hyōhō Niten Ichi-ryū employs it as a manual of technique and philosophy.

Musashi strove to be as great a master in Japanese calligraphy just as much as he did in swordsmanship. Musashi establishes a "no-nonsense" theme throughout the text. For instance, he repeatedly remarks that technical flourishes are excessive, and contrasts worrying about such things with the principle that all technique is simply a method of cutting down one's opponent. He also continually makes the point that the understandings expressed in the book are important for combat on any scale, whether a one-on-one duel or a massive battle. Descriptions of principles are often followed by admonitions to "investigate this thoroughly" through practice rather than trying to learn them by merely reading.

Though ideas are taken from other sources, the text is predominantly seminal. The five "books" refer to the idea that there are different elements of battle, just as there are different physical elements in life, as described by Buddhism, Shinto, and other Eastern religions.

The five books are Musashi's descriptions of the exact methods or techniques that are described by such elements.

The term *Ichi School* refers to "Niten No Ichi Ryu" or "Ni-Ten Ichi Ryu", which literally translates to "Two Heavens, One School". Alternative translations include: "Two Swords, One Spirit", and "Two Swords, One Entity". The translation, "Two Swords, One Dragon" was thought to be a misinterpretation of the Kanji word Ryu.

- The Book of Earth chapter serves as an introduction and metaphorically discusses martial arts, leadership, and training as building a house.
- The Book of Water chapter describes Musashi's style, Ni-ten ichi-ryu, or "Two Heavens, One Style". It describes some basic techniques and fundamental principles.
- The Book of Fire chapter refers to the heat of battle and discusses matters such as different types of timing.
- The Book of Wind chapter is something of a pun since the Japanese character for "wind" can also mean "style" (such as, in martial arts). It discusses what Musashi considers to be the failings of various contemporary schools of sword fighting.
- The Book of the Void chapter is a short epilogue, describing, in more esoteric terms, Musashi's (probably) Zen-influenced thoughts on consciousness and the correct mindset.

The Earth book,[1] according to "Go Rin No Sho", refers expressly to the strategy taught by Musashi at the Ichi School. It is said to be how to distinguish the Way through "Sword-Fencing", or "Swordsmanship". The idea of strategy would be encouraged to be very astute in their study and strategy. Know the smallest things and the biggest things, the shallowest things and the deepest things. As if it were a straight road mapped out on the ground... These things cannot be explained in detail. From one thing, know ten thousand things. When you attain the Way of Strategy there will not be one thing you cannot see. You must study hard.

Upon their mastery of the strategy and timing listed in the five books, Musashi states that people will be able to defeat ten men as easily as they could defeat one, and asks: "When you have reached this point, will it not mean that you are invincible?"

The strategies listed in this discipline or book relate to situations requiring different weapons and tactics, such as indoor weapons.

Musashi states that the use of <u>glaive</u>-like <u>naginata</u> and <u>spears</u> are purely for the field, whereas the longsword and accompanying shortsword can be used in most environments, such as on horseback or in a fierce battle. Musashi also remarks on the <u>gun</u> as having no equal on the battlefield, until swords clash, when it becomes useless. He does note that the gun had the disadvantage of being unable to see a bullet and adjust aim as one would with a bow. He writes: "The bow is tactically strong at the commencement of battle, especially battles on a moor, as it is possible to shoot quickly from among the spearmen. However, it is unsatisfactory in sieges, or when the enemy is more than forty yards away.

In The Book of Five Rings, he writes on timing:

Timing is important in dancing and pipe or string music, for they are in rhythm only if the timing is good. Timing and rhythm are also involved in the military arts, shooting bows and guns, and riding horses. In all skills and abilities, there is timing.... There is timing in the whole life of the warrior, in his thriving and declining, in his harmony and discord. Similarly, there is timing in the Way of the merchant, in the rise and fall of capital. All things entail rising and falling timing. You must be able to discern this. In strategy, there are various timing considerations. From the outset, you must know the applicable timing and the inapplicable timing, and from among the large and small things and the fast and slow timings find the relevant timing, first seeing the distance timing and the background timing. This is the main thing in strategy. It is especially important to know the background timing, otherwise your strategy will become uncertain.

The Book of Earth ends with nine basic principles – the "ground" upon which the samurai must rely. These are "practical" or "worldly," each intended to help develop an understanding of strategy (while the other books focus on tactics and movement). These rules are for his students and are complemented by the 21 "spiritual principles" for all to follow, which are found in the <u>Dokkōdō</u> (Musashi's final work). The principles are:

1. "Do not think dishonestly."
2. "The Way is in training."
3. "Become acquainted with every art."
4. "Know the Ways of all professions."
5. "Distinguish between gain and loss in worldly matters."
6. "Develop an intuitive judgment and understanding for everything."
7. "Perceive those things which cannot be seen."
8. "Pay attention even to trifles."
9. "Do nothing which is of no use."

THE BOOK OF WATER

The Book of Water concerns <u>strategy</u>, <u>spirituality</u> and philosophy. The meaning of water in relation to life is flexibility. Water demonstrates natural flexibility as it changes to conform with the boundaries that contain it, seeking the most efficient and productive path. So also should one possess the ability to change in accordance with one's own situation to easily shift between disciplines, methods, and options when presented with new information. A person should master many aspects of life allowing them to possess both balance and flexibility.

The spiritual bearing in strategy, which Musashi writes about concerns your temperament and spirituality whilst in the midst of, or in formulation of a battle. Being a Buddhist, most of what is written in the section concerning spirituality refers to principles of calmness, tranquillity and spiritual balance:

In strategy, your spiritual bearing must not be any different from normal. Both in fighting and in everyday life you should be determined though calm.

This balance refers to what could be thought of as yin and yang within one person. The over-familiarity or over-use of one weapon is discouraged by Musashi, as it would be seen to reveal one's spirituality to one's enemy. The idea is that a perfectly balanced spirit is also a perfectly balanced physical presence, and neither creates weakness nor reveals it to an enemy.

During battle, spirituality and balance are something of which Musashi notes that one should take advantage. Since small people know the spirituality of big people, they can thus note differences and weaknesses between each other. This is something that seems easy, but it is said to change when one is on the battlefield, as then one must know to both adjust one's spiritual balance according to the surrounding environment and to perceive the balance of others to take advantage accordingly.

Just as one's spirit should be balanced, one's various techniques be honed to a perfectly balanced demeanour. In terms of stance, much like balance within the trooper, Musashi notes that stance is an important part of strategy or battle: *Adopt a* stance with the head erect, neither hanging down, nor looking up, nor twisted. This is part of what Musashi notes as wedging in.

In regard to the gaze of someone, he notes that a person must be able to perceive that which is all around him without moving their eyeballs noticeably, which is said to be a skill that takes an enormous amount of practice to perfect. He notes that this is again one of the most important parts of strategy as well as being able to see things that are close, such as the technique of an enemy. It is also used to perceive things far away, such as arriving troops or enemies, as that is the precursor to battle. One can then change one's actions according to what one sees.

Attitudes of Swordsmanship:

Upper

Middle

Lower

Right Side

Left Side

The five attitudes of swordsmanship are referred to as the five classifications of areas for attack on the human body. These are areas that are noted for their advantages when striking at an enemy, and the strategist is said to think of them when in situations where, for any reason, they should not be able to strike them and adjust accordingly.

Your attitude should be large or small according to the situation. Upper, Lower and Middle attitudes are decisive. Left-side and right-side attitudes are fluid. Left and Right attitudes should be used if there is an obstruction overhead or to one side. The decision to use Left or Right depends on the place.

As each is thought of as an attitude, it could be thought of that Musashi means to practice with each "attitude" so that you do not become over-reliant upon one, something which Musashi repeatedly notes as being worse than bad technique.

"No Attitude" refers to those strategists who do not go with the use of the "Five Attitudes" and prefer to simply go without the attitudes of the long sword to focus entirely on technique, as opposed to focusing on both technique and the five attitudes. This is similar to taking chances as opposed to making chances.

The attitude of "Existing – Non Existing", mixes the Five Attitudes with the Attitude of "No Attitude", meaning that the user of the longsword uses the techniques and principles of both at whichever moment is most opportune.

"In-One Timing" refers to the technique of biding one's time until a suitable gap can be found in the enemies' defense, to which one will deliver one fatal blow to the enemy. Although this is said to be difficult, Musashi notes that masters of this technique are usually masters of the five attitudes because they must be perceptive of weaknesses. It is rumoured that Musashi disgraced a former sword master by using such a technique with a <u>bokken</u>, but there are no descriptions mentioning "In one" timing.

"Abdomen Timing of Two" refers to <u>feinting</u> an attack, then striking an enemy as they are retreating from the attack, hitting them in the abdomen with the correct timing of either two moves or two seconds. Although the technique seems relatively simple, Musashi lists this as one of the hardest techniques to time correctly.

"No Design, No Conception" refers to when words and actions are spontaneously the same. Aside from this philosophical approach to the meaning, the technique is relatively simple to explain: if you are in a deadlock with the enemy, using the force from the cut, you push with your body and use the disciplines outlined in the Void Book to knock the enemy over.

This is the most important method of hitting. It is often used. You must train hard to understand it.

The "Flowing Water Cut" technique is relevant to a fight with an enemy of a similar level in swordsmanship. When attacking fast, Musashi notes that one will always be at a stalemate, so like stagnant water, one must cut as slowly as possible with the long sword. At the beginning of this technique, both combatants will be searching for an opening within each other's defence. When the opponent either tries to push off the sword or to hasten back as to disengage it, you must first expand your whole body and your mind. By moving your body first and then that of your sword, you will be able to strike powerfully and broadly with a movement that seems to reflect the natural flow of water. Ease and confidence will be attained when this technique is continuously practised.

"Continuous Cut" refers to when you are again faced with stalemate within a duel, where your swords are clasped together. In one motion, when your sword springs away from theirs, Musashi says to use a continuous motion to slash their head, body, and legs. "Fire and Stone's Cut" refers to when swords clash together. Without raising the sword, cut as strongly as possible. This means cutting quickly with hands, body, and legs.

"Red Leaves Cut" refers to knocking down the enemy's long sword in the spirit of the "No Design, No Conception" cut.[citation needed]

THE BOOK OF FIRE

The *Fire Book* refers to fighting methods unlike the specific fighting techniques listed in the *Water Book*. It goes into a broader scope in terms of hints to assess a situation, as well as specific situational instructions.

He notes the obvious advantages of armour and preparedness before a duel or battle as it applies to one man or a whole group of men:

As one man can defeat ten men, so can one thousand men defeat ten thousand. However, you can become a master of strategy by training alone with a sword, so that you can understand the enemy's stratagems, his strength and resources, and come to appreciate how to apply strategy to beat ten thousand enemies.

The dependence on location according to the *Go Rin No Sho* is crucial. You must be in a place where man-made objects such as buildings, towers, castles, and such do not obstruct your view, as well as facing or standing in a position where the sun or moon does not affect your vision. This is purely so that your vision is focused on nothing but the enemy, and thus there is more concentration upon the enemy's stratagems. Musashi also seems to note the age-old strategy of the High Ground:

You must look down on the enemy, and take up your attitude on slightly higher places. Other kinds of tactics Musashi tells are a way of ensuring that the enemy is at a disadvantage. Forcing yourself on the non-dominant side of a trooper is one way because the left side is difficult for a right-handed soldier. Other disadvantages, such as forcing enemies into footholds, swamps, ditches, and other difficult terrain, force the enemy to be uncertain of his situation.

These things cannot be clearly explained in words. You must research what is written here. In these three ways of forestalling, you must judge the situation. This does not mean that you always attack first; but if the enemy attacks first you can lead him around. In strategy, you have effectively won when you forestall the enemy, so you must train well to attain this.

Ken No Sen (Attacking) is the most obvious method of forestalling an enemy because a head-on collision forces both parties to a standstill. Although it is not mentioned, Musashi must have been well aware that this method would also be the most likely to have a higher death count than the others due to the sheer mass of enemies because more than one enemy could then attack a single soldier or trooper.

As the name suggests, *Tai No Sen* (Waiting for the Initiative) is invented for very opportunistic and decided battles between parties. The main idea is to feign weakness to open a weak spot, or <u>Achilles' heel</u>, in the opposing force, and then regroup to exploit such a hole by attacking deep within the enemy's party. Although it is not mentioned, this would most likely be to kill the officer of the highest rank as an attempt to remove the tactical centre of a group of soldiers. A method particularly useful for Musashi or others, if attacking a general directly would signal the end of the battle upon his defeat.

Only a small amount of text is written about Tai Tai No Sen (Accompanying and Forestalling). Albeit very confusing, the idea of Tai Tai No Sen is circumventing an ambush or quick attack from the enemy by taking the initiative and attacking in full force. Musashi admits that this is a difficult thing to explain.

Although there are other methods, they are mostly situational methods relating to the crossing of rough terrain, and battling within such rough terrain. Although it spreads over two or more paragraphs, most information is common sense, relating to caution and avoidance of such situations.

The idea of timing, as with singular battles, is known as the most important part of attacking next to the skill of participants. However, the type of timing in this instance is somewhat different from the timing noted in *The Ground Book* since this variety of timing requires looking at the various physical factors that affect an enemy during battle, such as determining if strength is waning or rising within a group of troopers.

The idea of treading down the sword is a very simple technique. Squashing an enemy's attack before it starts by using a form of charging and then attacking under the veil of gunpowder smoke, and arrow fire, the initial attacks used when starting battles can be highly effective. Individually, it refers to attacking the enemy's sword, breaking it, removing it from play, and a technique of controlling it through direct blade-on-blade contact.

Just as Musashi mentions in his philosophical style, there is a cause for a collapse. As there is a collapse within an enemy, such as waning in his numbers, Musashi notes that one must observe such events and use them to advantage.

He notes that an enemy's formation can fall if they lose rhythm. It was known that in such battles, drummers drummed a tune for their other fellow soldiers to march to; and, if the rhythm was lost, it led to a "collapse when their rhythm becomes deranged".

THE BOOK OF WIND

Whereas most of the information given in the previous books is useful in such a way that it could still be applicable today, this book is primarily concerned with the specific details about other strategies that existed at the time. The broader lesson from this book is that an important part of understanding one's own way is to understand the way of one's opponent as precisely as possible.

Musashi notes that although most schools have secret and ancient strategies, most forms are derivative of other martial arts. Their similarities and differences evolved through situational factors, such as indoor or outdoor duelling, and the style adapted to the school. He indicates that his appraisal may be one-sided because the only school he had an interest in was his own, and, in a way, he does not see parallels to his own creation and work. However, he still admits that without a basic understanding of these alternate techniques, one will not be able to learn *Ni Ten Ichi Ryu*, probably for reasons of finding the wrongs in other techniques and righting them within yourself in *Ni Ten Ichi Ryu*.

The main difference that Musashi notes between the Ichi School and other strategists and schools is that other schools do not teach the "broader" meaning of strategy. There is a strategy above sword-fencing: "Some of the world's strategists are concerned only with sword-fencing, and limit their training to flourishing the long sword and carriage of the body." The book has many paragraphs on the subject of other schools' techniques, and much of the text lists the ways that other schools do not conform to the ideals that he himself writes about in the *Book of Five Rings*, such as footwork, sight, and over-reliance or over-familiarity with a weapon.

The Book of Void

Although short, the void book lists, philosophically, the nature of both human knowledge and other things. The void book expressly deals with "That which cannot be seen".

By knowing things that exist, you can know that which does not exist.

The Book of Nothing, according to Musashi, is the true meaning of the strategy of Ni Ten Ichi Ryu. It seems very esoteric in nature because he emphasizes that people must learn to perceive that which they cannot understand or comprehend. He notes that in this Void, what can be comprehended are things that we do and see, such as the way of the warrior, martial arts, and *Ni Ten Ichi Ryu*. At the same time, in the Void, things we do not do or see (which he calls *Spirit*) are part of the information that we perceive on a conscious level, but with which we have no physical relationship. It is arguable whether Musashi is referring to religious spirituality or if he is actually explaining a way to live a life and to process thoughts.

In the void is virtue, and no evil. Wisdom has existence, principle has existence, the Way has existence, and spirit is nothingness.

In the above quote, Musashi speaks of "virtue and no evil". This may mean "goodness and banishment of evil" or "purpose and non-existence of good and evil", and the exact meaning is open to debate.

Since Musashi is drawing upon classical Buddhist Five Element theory, Void, in this case, refers to Sunyata (in Pali), sometimes translated as "Emptiness", or "ether". Void, as such, is also empty of the sense of self (anatta), good and evil, wanting and non-wanting, and is the spiritual dynamic that forms the jumping-off point to satori, enlightenment. Emptiness, and the establishing of the conditions that allow it to arise, is a common theme in Zen Buddhist meditation practice, which informed the perspective of the author.

You may be asking why "The Book of Rings" is at all relevant in context with the Law of Attraction. Life is full of conflicts and even in 2024 we still have wars and conflicts worldwide. Dealing with any conflict takes thought, preparation, planning and execution whether it be a physical war the guns or swords or a mental war with words and deeds. "The Book of Rings" discusses how warriors prepare for battle and when I am in a trading competition and often read excerpts from this book to inspire and motivate me. I am calm, serene and sure when I start my chart analysis.

CHAPTER 10

THE UNIVERSE WILL TEST YOU FOR THE NEXT STEP – BE PREPARED

I want you to consider why it sometimes seems that the universe is testing you.

Just when you think you are on the right path and you feel great, something negative or undesirable materializes in your circumstance and you ask yourself what the hell did I do to deserve this! This has happened to me on a number of occasions and as I write "Think Link Create" a big challenge to my faith and belief has indeed appeared, almost like the Universe knew I was going to write this. I believe the Universe, God, divine mind, The Tao (The Tao that can be named is really not the Tao as I explained earlier in the book) have a sense of humour like us humans do. When this challenge appeared a few weeks ago I smiled, looked up and said "Thank You, I am ready to move forward".

In previous years as I look back, before I was aware of the Law of Attraction and the Universal Mind, I would go into deep depression feeling the world and God were against me.

How wrong I was and thank goodness I did not attempt to take my life, because at times, especially in the nineties I was at rock bottom, heavily reliant on alcohol (I never smoked or took drugs, if I did I wouldn't be here today!!)

For many who deliberately align their intentions to focus on their dream, the path to manifestation isn't always easy or direct. The Universe seems to throw up distractions and detours as if to stop you in your tracks and challenge your preparedness for the world you seek. To manifest. But rather than simply testing your resolve, what if these speed bumps were about providing opportunities for you to show that you are sincerely committed to welcoming great change. What if these steps are actually designed to test your readiness to accept the treasures to come?

The reality is that you can only unlock your future desires by conquering the trials of your present. The whole idea of manifesting your future and creating space for your deepest desires and dreams to come true is truly magical. It really should not come as any surprise that there will be obstacles in this mystical adventure, many challenges to success and questions needing to be answered. What really sustains the art of manifesting? Why do so many stumble on this path? Manifestation is, at its heart, the merging of intention and alignment. That union is strong and powerful, but it can be hit by unexpected waves of challenges. In these times, it can seem that the universe is presenting you with the opposite of your desire. It can indeed be unnerving when you choose goals that embrace positivity. Creating wealth, good health, happiness and new opportunities or inspiring connections. Instead, find yourself caught up in circumstances that contradict your strongest intentions.

This web of obstacles and distractions constrain your finances, deplete your motivation, impact your health and fracture connections. If left unresolved, these experiences can multiply the challenges you face and cast doubt on the course you have chosen. This is not a time to abandon your dream. Even as you wonder why the tide of change has turned so quickly, you must remain firm in your dreams. You must realize that the universe has a unique way to prepare you for what's to come. In essence, the universe is testing your commitment and authenticity, seeking to question whether your desires come from your heart. And if you are genuinely prepared to embrace the reality you seek, are you ready for what you seek to manifest? The desire for immense wealth is a common aspiration, and the journey to financial abundance requires a transformation just like any other. It is not unexpected that the universe will create challenges designed to test whether you are the type of person who can accept and embrace this responsibly. The universe

THE UNIVERSE WILL TEST YOU FOR THE NEXT STEP-BE PREPARED

will test you and make you question if you are really ready to walk this life-changing path. The tests of the universe reflect the depth of your desires and ask if you are ready to embrace the nature of your dreams. When you understand how to navigate the trials of the universe, you will discover that they are mere stepping stones taking you closer to the treasures you are looking for.

As the things, circumstances and good fortune you desire begin to materialize your path will change, and you will be encouraged to further find your truest self and embrace your desires. As you go deeper, you will inevitably come back to a fundamental question that lies at the heart of manifestation. This is a question that holds the keys to unlocking the mysteries of the universe. What if manifestation is not about the universe fulfilling our specific request, but something deeper What if it's about the universe reflecting yourself? What if the universe is not a wish-fulfilling entity, but a mirror that reflects our essence? Manifestation is not about receiving exactly what you ask for, but it is instead about receiving what aligns with who you are.

No desire to get rich or to find deep love will manifest if your inner self remains unchanged. If you continue to resonate to the same frequency, then change will not happen. This change in understanding is fundamental. The universe is not an adversary but rather is the sculptor of your journey. When the universe throws up challenges, see it as an invitation to transform and change your perspective. Ask yourself, are you prepared to mirror the energy of abundance, even in the face of obstacles? Only when you appreciate this perspective will you see the opportunities in the midst of challenges. This profound transformation in your mindset will bring you to yet another realization. It is the universe's intention to witness your commitment to your newfound self, especially in times of adversity. By declaring your commitment to manifestation, you are opting for a reinvention, choosing a new version of yourself. It is this new reimagined self.

That the universe will sculpt and gently guide you to live as the person who has already overcome many challenges along your journey, it is fundamental that we acknowledge that every time we embark on a manifestation we are choosing to embrace a new version of ourselves. When the process of manifestation encounters obstacles and becomes more challenging, it is often a sign that your old self is rebelling against this transformation. Take comfort by knowing that this resistance also means the new you is about to emerge to navigate trials set by the universe. You need to first greet the reinvention of yourself with a sense of gratitude and even joy. When you start to see your old patterns and self-image begin to crumble, take comfort in knowing that the new you is coming. Many people can be frightened by deep spiritual and personal change. They fear the unknown and the loss of the old. And so at a pivotal moment, may retreat to old patterns. It is vital to acknowledge this at the time it is happening. That rebellion from the old self is a forerunner to change only by grasping and embracing this upheaval. Can you gain the courage for metamorphosis? Only when the old self falls apart and dissolves. Can you Undertake a remarkable journey of evolution? Now is also the time to become the new version of yourself you seek to manifest. By taking on the attributes of the new, you will be able to resist focusing on scarcity and complaining. Your involved mindset will respond differently, with a sense of abundance and security, and you will not recoil from challenges. But instead, consider how to best deal with these situations. Inhabit and exercise the wisdom of experience to overcome fears, obstacles and tests. Learn to celebrate your transformative progress by considering every small step as a triumph on your path to manifestation. Understand that transformation is not instantaneous but is a gradual daily evolution. And that every sunrise allows you to engage in your growth.

When you celebrate each step forward and every small achievement or victory, you send a message to your subconscious. Which reinforces the notion that you are making progress? Rather than aim for instant transformations, embrace your time and respect each step of your unique journey. Acknowledge that every small step paves the way for remarkable changes. And that you are building a bridge between where you are and where you want to be. Understand that when a challenge arises and things don't seem to line up, you are being asked to reorder your thoughts and energy. To allow growth you celebrate victories, big and small, knowing that the universe is taking note.

THE UNIVERSE WILL TEST YOU FOR THE NEXT STEP-BE PREPARED

It sees your dedication and your commitment to transformation, and in turn, it responds by aligning circumstances with your intentions. This is where the art of manifesting truly flourishes. Manifestation is not about perfection or overnight changes. Manifestation is about consistent progress in embracing your journey on this wonderful planet we call home.

Dear friends, remember the universe is ever-vigilant, and that it recognizes your efforts and harmonizes with your intentions, know that you are, in fact, the architect of your own journey. You have the power to do things that seemed impossible one hundred years ago. We have been to space, to the bottom of one of the deepest trenches in the ocean, piloted by the director of Avitar, the great James Cameron.

If You can Think, Link (to the source energy force) then you WILL create, it is your birth right, embrace the journey because you may have been here in the past and may revisit in the future.

As I sign off after nearly twelve years of trying to write and publish Think, Link, Create I instinctively know that this is the right time as I approach my fifty-eighth birthday!!

I am so very blessed to have a wonderful family, great customers at my trading software company, TradeGuider Systems, and to live in one of the most beautiful parts of the United Kingdom, the New Forest National Park in a seventeenth-century cottage complete with a well as you can see below.

The well was constructed and 1706 and is still working today, not that I would ever drink the water!

One customer who visited me at my home for one-to-one training using our trading software and strategies commented that this must be a wishing well and he was very serious.

He explained as follows, although I have gone into a bit more detail having done some history on my well.

He said "Gavin, A wishing well is a term from European folklore to describe wells where it was thought that any spoken wish would be granted. The idea that a wish would be granted came from the notion that water housed deities or had been placed there as a gift from the gods. This practice is thought to have arisen because water is a source of life and was often a scarce commodity.

The Germanic and Celtic peoples considered springs and wells sacred places. Sometimes the places were marked with wooden statues possibly of the god associated with the pool. Germanic peoples were known to throw the armour and weapons of defeated enemies into bogs and other pools of water as offerings to their gods. As water is necessary for life, wells became popular places not only to get life-sustaining water but also as a social area. This has now related to town centres having wells in the centre of them. Water was also seen to have healing powers, and wells became popular, with many people drinking the water, bathing in it, or simply wishing over it. Some people believed that the guardians or dwellers of the well would grant them their wish if they paid a price.

After uttering the wish, one would generally drop coins in the well. The wish would then be granted by the guardian or dweller based on how the coin would land at the bottom of the well. If the coin landed heads up, the guardian of the well would grant the wish, but the wish of a tails-up coin would be ignored. It was thus potentially lucky to throw coins in the well, but it depended on how they landed.

Since 2021, excavation of an ancient wooden wishing well has been underway in what is now the town of Germering, Bavaria, Germany. More than 13,500 artefacts have been found, dating from the Bronze Age to the early Middle Ages.

The Celtic clootie well tradition and the English well-dressing tradition appear to be related to this kind of ancient well veneration. The tradition of dropping pennies in ponds and fountains also stems from this. Coins would be placed there as gifts for the deity to show appreciation.

The belief that deities inhabited wells in Germanic and Celtic traditions may be a leftover from ancient mythology such as Mímir's Well from Nordic myths, also known as the "Well of Wisdom", a well that could grant the wisher infinite wisdom provided they sacrificed something they held dear. Odin was asked to sacrifice his right eye which he threw into the well to receive not only the wisdom of seeing the future but the understanding of why things must be. Mímir is the Nordic god of wisdom, and his well sits at the roots of Yggdrasil, the World Tree which draws its water from the well.

Another theory is that people may have unknowingly discovered the <u>biocidal properties of both copper and silver</u>. The two metals are traditionally used in coins. Throwing coins made of either of these metals could help make the water safer to drink. Wells that were frequented by those who threw coins in may have been less affected by a range of bacterial infections making them seem more fortunate and may have even appeared to have cured people suffering from repeated infections.

When I arrived at my new home in January 2023, the first place the Estate Agent took my wife Laura and I too was the well. We began talking about making a wish and immediately I saw the connection between Think, Link, Create and wishing for a better life, happiness, more money, good fortune and good health and so when we moved in on 10th January 2023 I went to the well, threw in a pound coin and I had only one wish at that moment. Now I am told you are not supposed to tell people your wish until it manifests into your reality. My wish was very simple, very emotionally charged and very directed at Source, the universe which governs us.

My Wish:

Please Lord grant me a wish that can be fulfilled quickly and effortlessly with your guidance, encouragement and Love. I have been trying to write and publish my third book since 2012, twelve years in the making. I have learnt a great deal in those years, travelling to 17 countries and experiencing multiple cultures and beliefs, but nearly all lead to You. Please, I wish to finish Think, Link, Create by December 1^{st,} 2024 and have the book published by a professional publishing house that can guide me through the process of reaching out to millions of like-minded people who are ready for their awakening. I am truly grateful for the great life I have and continue to have.

I commend this powerful wish to You Lord as I drop this new one-pound coin into my well. Thank You, Thank You, Thank You.

The rest is history as You will read this book.

Be careful what you wish for, the universe is always listening and very receptive to positive intentions and thoughts.

Make your wish or wishes today, write them down, you do not need a well to make the wishes and dreams a reality. You are all-powerful, a mystery of nature, a creature of God. We are all one whether we choose to believe that or not.

CHAPTER 11

USE POSITIVE WORDS/AFFIRMATIONS TO GET POSITIVE RESULTS – COMMAND YOUR INNER VOICE – I AM....

The two words "I AM" have very powerful meaning to both the conscious and subconscious mind.

The phrase "I AM THAT I AM" has a very significant spiritual meaning:

- It represents the concept of ultimate self-identity and the recognition of the eternal nature of the soul.
- It signifies that one's true essence is not bound by the limitations of the physical body.
- It symbolizes the divine essence within each individual, commonly referred to as the soul or higher self.
- Some interpret it as a call to self-realization and personal empowerment.

WHAT ARE POSITIVE AFFIRMATIONS?

Affirmations are positive, present-tense statements of confirmation, validity, and belief.

Your own affirmations are powerful tools that declare to your subconscious mind and the universe what you hold to be true and possible about yourself and the world.

Beware, however, as affirmations work both ways. In fact, we are constantly using affirmations, whether we realize it or not.

Our thought processes impact our beliefs, and our beliefs impact our behaviour. Therefore, your thoughts and beliefs often end up dictating how you respond to the things in your daily life, even if you don't realize it.

Most people tend to unconsciously affirm the opposite of what they want and intend to create.

For example, they may repeat unhelpful thoughts like, **"I don't have enough money"** or, **"I don't deserve that"** or, **"I feel miserable"** continuing to affirm those undesired results.

In order to create your best life and step into the full potential of a new reality the first step is to tap into the power of affirmations. After all, if you're already unconsciously affirming negative thoughts, wouldn't you rather use that same energy to create positive change?

I once heard that the universe's only response to our requests is, *"Yes."*

So no matter what we ask for with our thoughts, attention, and vibration, whether unconsciously or deliberately, the universe is always granting our wishes.

Daily affirmations are a powerful way to boldly state to the universe what you intend to attract and create.

WHAT IS THE PURPOSE OF POSITIVE AFFIRMATIONS? DO THEY REALLY WORK?

It might be difficult to believe that a simple statement could play such a significant role when it comes to manifesting better things in our lives. When

I started using affirmations before going to sleep and again when I woke up it had a profound effect on my life. I have mentioned in previous chapters the power of words and the inner voice, so if your inner voice keeps telling you everything is great, the world is a wonderful place, I see beauty in the fields, the mountains, the rivers and the meadows and I know that the source power that created all this is in me, around me and serves me now.

Not only are positive affirmations a great way to work with the Law of Attraction but the impact of affirmations when it comes to making life changes and supporting personal growth has also been well-documented.

In fact, recent medical and scientific studies showed that practising self-affirmation in the form of positive mantras activated neural pathways associated with increasing self-worth and lowering stress.

Researchers also found that affirmations can predict positive changes in behaviour. In other words, people who used affirmations were more likely to successfully make changes in their behaviour, leading to long-term, positive life changes!

Proven Benefits of Affirmations

- Affirmations decrease stress, even in the face of negative experiences.
- Affirmations decrease resistance and defensiveness and support a positive perspective of challenges.
- Affirmations can contribute to academic achievement and career success.
- Affirmations lessen the amount of time spent ruminating on negative thoughts, helping individuals stay in the present moment.
- Affirmations empower people to be more resilient during difficult times.
- Affirmations increase optimism, hope, and a sense of possibility for the future.
- Affirmations increase feelings of self-worth and self-love.

Easy Ways to Incorporate Daily Positive Affirmations into Your Daily Life:

Start your mornings with daily positive affirmations: Doing this simple practice first thing in the morning will set you up for success and infuse you with positive energy to face the new day with hope and optimism.

Use affirmations throughout your day: As you face challenges, demands, and stress throughout the day, call a mental timeout. Take a deep breath and spend a minute or two reciting positive affirmations to enter the next phase of your day in a state of clarity.

Say affirmations as you transition from work to home: Stop and affirm the experience you want to create, how you want to interact with your family, and the good things you desire for the rest of your day.

End your day with positive affirmations: It's a great way to end your evening on a high note of positivity, gratitude, and optimism. Affirmations have been shown to decrease stress and improve sleep!)

Here are just some of the most popular affirmations, all of which I use at different times and in different circumstances, I hope that you try using these because the results which are positive manifest extremely quickly.

Positive Morning Affirmations to Start Your Day

- All that's possible for anyone is possible for me.
- I am supported by a power greater than me, that is breathing me right now.
- I attract positive things and people in my life each day.
- I choose to do great things today.
- Every day I discover interesting and exciting new paths to pursue.
- New opportunities are attracted to me every day.

- I am well rested and energized, excited to take on the day.
- I am grateful for the gift of waking up this morning.
- I make decisions that support my best and highest good.
- I am the architect of my life, and today is my best day yet.

Daily Positive Affirmations

- I am worthy and deserving of all the things I would love in my life.
- My ideas are valuable and worth being shared.
- I do what I can, from where I am, with what I have.
- I am enough and I am loved.
- I am far more powerful and contain more potential than any circumstance, situation, or condition.
- I am connected to a deep well of inner wisdom and guidance that gives me confidence.
- I am manifesting my dream job and am excited for the new opportunity that is already coming to me.
- I am capable. There is no failure, only an invitation to a new way of doing things.
- I am a creative force. I am inspired by the universe and open to new ideas.
- I am focused and my mind is clear.

Positive Affirmations for Women

- I am safe in all my relationships, and I openly give and receive love.
- My life is free from clutter and drama. My organization creates the flow of abundance in my life.

- Every day, in every way I am getting better and better.
- I choose to have compassion for my mistakes and create my personal best TODAY!
- My body responds to my healing thoughts, and I radiate health & vitality.
- I am worthy of love and I am always attracting supportive relationships into my life.
- My future is bright and I am not limited by my past.
- I deserve to invest in myself at the highest level.
- I am powerful and confident. The people around me can feel it.
- I choose to be kind to myself today and every day.

Positive Affirmations for Children

- I am strong. I am smart. I work hard.
- I am beautiful. I am respectful.
- I am amazing. I am great.
- If I fall, I get back up.
- I choose to learn and grow. I take baby steps to create my personal best TODAY.
- I can do hard things.
- I am safe.
- I am not alone.
- I am loved.
- I am kind and others are kind to me.

WORDS/AFFIRMATIONS TO GET POSITIVE RESULTS-COMMAND YOUR INEER VOICE-I AM……

Positive Affirmations for Men

- I am strong and capable.
- It is safe to feel and express my emotions to those who care about me.
- I choose to find something good in every day.
- I am accomplishing my goals each and every day.
- Today I choose to embody my personal best in all things I do.
- I find a positive perspective in every situation.
- Creative solutions always come to me easily.
- I overcome obstacles with ease. I am resilient.
- I choose motivation and inspiration over stress.
- I am supported in all ways.

Positive Affirmations for Work

- I am grateful for my job and all the things it affords me.
- I finish what matters and let go of what doesn't.
- My work matters. My contributions are important.
- I have every quality I need to achieve success.
- I am surrounded by people who want to see me succeed.
- I am prepared, confident, and collaborative.
- Unexpected solutions come to me whenever I need them.
- I always do my best and it is seen and appreciated.
- My success is inevitable.
- Today is an opportunity for greatness.

Positive Affirmations for Relationships

- I am worthy of a healthy relationship.
- I deserve love exactly as I am.
- The right relationship is already on its way to me.
- I am excited and curious about the people I will meet today.
- The love I seek is also seeking me.
- I am happy and content in all my relationships.
- I am seen, heard, and valued in all of my relationships.
- My love for my partner grows with each passing day, as their love for me also grows each day.
- I am grateful to be in a loving, committed, strong relationship.
- I am loveable and I am surrounded by love every day.

Positive Affirmations for Anxiety

- I am calm and at peace.
- I choose positive thoughts and positive outcomes for myself.
- I am safe and supported now and always.
- I can do the best I can with what I have right now. I don't have to worry about anything else.
- I choose to trust the process of life.
- I choose to remember that I'm okay, even if part of me doesn't feel sure yet.
- I feel calmer with each breath I take in. My body relaxes with each breath I release.
- I am in control of my day. I am in control of my life.

- I am more than my anxious thoughts.
- Every cell of my body is filled with peace and tranquillity.

Positive Affirmations to End the Day

- I am grateful for the experiences, connections, and growth this day brought me.
- I am proud of myself for doing my best today.
- I release any worry from today and choose calm and relaxation in this present moment.
- I am grateful for today and looking forward to an even better tomorrow.
- I choose rest and relaxation. I am calm and at peace.
- I trust that today is bringing me closer to achieving my dreams.
- My body, mind, and spirit are completely renewed as I sleep.
- I am at peace with today and excited for tomorrow.
- No matter what I accomplished today, I choose to remember that my worth is not defined by achievements.
- I have restful, restorative sleep and I wake up feeling fully rested and vibrant.

Positive Affirmations for Manifesting

- I am a powerful creator and I am creating the life of my dreams.
- I am grateful for the countless opportunities that come to me every day.
- I take every action remembering that I am worthy of receiving the life of my dreams.

WORDS/AFFIRMATIONS TO GET POSITIVE RESULTS-COMMAND YOUR INEER VOICE-I AM……

- God and the Universe are working in my favour at every turn.
- I am grateful for all that I have even as I am receiving even more than I ever thought possible.
- I make brave and empowered choices because I know I am always supported.
- My intuition guides me to take inspired action in the direction of my dreams.
- I am co-creating an abundant life with God and the Universe.
- I receive everything I need in perfect, divine timing.
- I am full of gratitude for my life and always experiencing new things to be grateful for.
- Use these affirmations every day after reading this book. Get into the habit of programming your conscious and subconscious mind with good, positive, happy vibrations brought about by your thoughts, words, and actions.

The most important two words I say to myself regularly is:

I AM

I am well, I am happy, I am healthy, I am prosperous, I am lucky, I am confident, I am peaceful, I am friendly, I am present in the moment, I am blessed, I abundant, I am serene, I am sure.

I AM GOD

I AM GOD

I AM GOD

WORDS/AFFIRMATIONS TO GET POSITIVE RESULTS-COMMAND YOUR INEER VOICE-I AM......

Because at the basic core, each and every one of us is just that. We are connected to the Source, the Divine Mind, the Higher Power. We are all one in a field of energy that created us and nurtures us if we so choose.

You can be host to God, or You can be hostage to your ego. It's Your choice Dr. Wayne Dyer told us and I repeat this yet again because it is true.

Read "Three Magic Words" by Uell S. Andersen and find the film of the same name and You will know what I and millions of others are now discovering in this "New Age" of change which is upon us.

Embrace this new area and fear nothing because there is nothing to fear.

Be strong, be resilient, be happy and be calm because life is a miracle, a gift from a source so enjoy every moment as you finish Think, Link, Create and move forward with optimism, joy and great vibes.

From my heart, I thank you for reading my book and I look forward to meeting you in person at one of my live seminars or at one of my many webinars planned for 2024-25.

As I conclude Think, Link, Create with mixed emotions I know in my heart that the next chapter in my incredible life journey has just begun as I approach my fifty-eighth birthday. They say life begins at forty, well maybe for me life begins again at fifty-eight!

I take this opportunity to send out my heartfelt thanks to everyone who has encouraged me to complete and publish Think, Link, Create. There are too many to thank individually but you know who you are because I probably sent you the manuscript!

I want to thank everyone who has been involved as either a customer or employee of my company formed in 1999, TradeGuider Systems International. (TradeGuider.Com

I especially want to thank my very special wife, Laura and my three children, Nathan, now twenty-four, Olivia now 15 and Ryan now fourteen. Without these rocks that have seen me go through some really challenging times to seeing a day like today where I am on top of the world, I realize the importance of family.

I have a very close inner circle of friends I have known for decades and they are my second family, there for me when I was down and always ready for a party. As I write this book I decided to quit drinking alcohol, not because it was a problem but because of a video I saw on YouTube by accident. (Actually, there is no such thing as knowledge accidentally falling in your lap, it is truly divine intervention because believe it or not the universe has got your back.) The video was produced and presented by James Swanwick, a former ESPN presenter who has now become an entrepreneur running several businesses. His website is www.alcoholfreelifestyle.com and many of the stories he shares I am sure many will relate to. Incidentally, since I quit drinking alcohol I have lost 22 pounds and my BMI is 22.3. My blood pressure is very good and my overall energy levels and enthusiasm through the roof.

I leave you these final words from the legend, the late Steve Jobs who was speaking to students at a graduation ceremony in California.

"When I was young, there was an amazing publication called the Whole Earth Catalogue, which was one of the bibles of my generation. It was created by a fellow named Stewart Brand, not far from here in Menlo Park and he brought it to life with his poetic touch. This was in the late sixties, before personal computers and desktop publishing, so it was all made with typewriters, scissors and Polaroid cameras. It was sort of like Google and paperback from 35 years before Google came along.

It was idealistic, overflowing with neat tools and great notions. Stuart and his team put out several issues of the Whole Earth Catalogue, and then when it ran its course, they put out a final issue. It was the mid-1970s, and I was your age. On the back cover of their final issue was a photograph of an early morning country road, the kind you might find yourself hitchhiking on if you were so adventurous. Beneath it were the words:

Stay hungry, Stay foolish. It was their farewell message as they signed off. Stay hungry, stay foolish and I have always wished that for myself, and now, as you graduate to begin anew, I wish that for you"

"Stay hungry. Stay foolish. Thank you all very much"

Great words and inspiration from a great man.

From my heart, I thank you for reading my book and I look forward to meeting you in person at one of my live seminars or at one of my many webinars planned for 2024.

May the universe and the power laws that it holds bring you health, happiness and lots of good fortune.

Whatever religion you follow or no religion at all, I say as the late Dave Allen, a famous UK comedian would say:

"May YOUR God bless you"

Namaste With Love,

Gavin

WWW.THINKLINKCREATE.COM

Recommended Further Reading and Study

- **Three Magic Words by Uell S. Andersen**
- **The Secret by Rhonda Byrne**
- **The Source by Dr. Sara Tara Swart**
- **Oneness With All Life by Eckhart Tolle**
- **The Biology of Belief by Bruce H. Lipton Ph.D.**
- **Think and Grow Rich by Napoleon Hill**
- **Outwitting The Devil by Napoleon Hill**
- **The Intention Experiment by Lynne McTaggart**
- **Mind To Matter by Dawson Church**
- **Ask And It Is Given By Esther and Jerry Hicks**
- **Getting Into The Vortex by Esther and Jerry Hicks**
- **The Seven Spiritual Laws Of Success by Deepak Chopra**

WORDS/AFFIRMATIONS TO GET POSITIVE RESULTS-COMMAND YOUR INEER VOICE-I AM……

- **The Book Of Five Rings by Miyamoto Musashi**
- **Unleash The Power Within By Tony Robbins**
- **I Am Not Your Guru By Tony Robbins**
- **The Science Of Getting Rich by Wallace Wattles**
- **Manifest – Seven Ways To Living Your Best Life by Roxie Nafousi**

WORDS/AFFIRMATIONS TO GET POSITIVE RESULTS-COMMAND YOUR INEER VOICE-I AM……

THE END

WORDS/AFFIRMATIONS TO GET POSITIVE RESULTS-COMMAND YOUR INEER VOICE-I AM……

- **The Book Of Five Rings by Miyamoto Musashi**
- **Unleash The Power Within By Tony Robbins**
- **I Am Not Your Guru By Tony Robbins**
- **The Science Of Getting Rich by Wallace Wattles**
- **Manifest – Seven Ways To Living Your Best Life by Roxie Nafousi**

WORDS/AFFIRMATIONS TO GET POSITIVE RESULTS-COMMAND YOUR INEER VOICE-I AM……

THE END

www.ingramcontent.com/pod-product-compliance
Lightning Source LLC
Chambersburg PA
CBHW081618100526
44590CB00021B/3487